How Will I Know Where I'm Going,
If I Don't Know Where I've Been?

How Will I Know Where I'm Going, If I Don't Know Where I've Been?

A Genealogical Journey

Elizabeth Ruderman Miller

authorHOUSE®

AuthorHouse™
1663 Liberty Drive
Bloomington, IN 47403
www.authorhouse.com
Phone: 1-800-839-8640

©2009 Elizabeth Ruderman Miller. All rights reserved.

No part of this book may be reproduced, stored in
a retrieval system, or transmitted by any means
without the written permission of the author.

First published by AuthorHouse   11/20/2009

ISBN: 978-1-4490-5104-4 (e)
ISBN: 978-1-4490-5103-7 (sc)

Library of Congress Control Number: 2009912332

Printed in the United States of America
Bloomington, Indiana

This book is printed on acid-free paper.

Author's Note

ENDURANCE IS ONE OF THE MOST DIFFICULT DISCIPLINES, BUT IT IS TO THE ONE WHO ENDURES THAT THE FINAL VICTORY COMES.
—BUDDAH

This is a story of hope, how-to and hard work.

Some lucky families have detailed histories overflowing with stories and pictures dating back hundreds of years. I barely knew anything about either side of my family, and like others had mistaken information which needed correcting.

I joined internet groups, wrote questions, researched time periods, and made numerous telephone calls trying to locate my family members. My suggestion to readers is NEVER consider a question too simple to ask the experts. Stay organized by setting up and keeping good files. Definitely,

KEEP AN OPEN MIND AND A GOOD SENSE OF HUMOR, because you never know what skeletons may be uncovered during your search. Finally, be patient and verify everything you discover if you plan to say it is the truth.

DON'T GIVE UP!!

Remember–you are solving a mystery–that is your challenge. Your genealogy may not be volumes, but it is yours. What you find are treasures to pass along to the next generations. I have more secrets to unravel, hopefully with the assistance of my newly found family members by my side. It is our shared past that makes us UNIQUE and FAMILY.

Dedication

To my incredible mother, Rose Hiller Ruderman whose mind and memory at the age of 95 were the inspiration for the genealogical journey I travelled for three years. May you read this now, over my shoulder with Daddy, and know how much I love you both.

To my new cousins, Pam and Bob Hoffman, whose friendship, sharing, caring, encouragement and "You go girl" about this project have meant so much.

To my wonderful husband, Roger, who put up with my endless hours researching and writing, successes and failures and who never once said, stop.

To Barbara Foster, who said "yes" when I asked her to assume the task of editing my work. You are a wonderful friend.

Thank you – I love and appreciate you all.

My Mother

Shortly before completing my manuscript, I lost my wonderful mother, Rose Hiller Ruderman on June 1, 2009 at age 95.

About twenty-five years ago, after a surgical procedure almost ended her life, I rushed to my Mom's hospital bedside. When she awakened from her coma, Mom told me of her 'near death' experience. She had seen my Dad peeking in from her hospital room doorway, only to have him smile and then vanish when she ventured toward him. In my heart, I knew Dad was telling her that he was waiting for her, but that it wasn't her time yet. She had far too much wisdom to impart.

During the following two plus decades, she counseled her children, grandchildren, great-grandchildren and friends. She never failed to 'tell it like is was', but her great gift was letting you know that she supported you and loved you, even if she disagreed with your choices.

She was one of a kind, and everyone whose life she touched was better for the experience.

The sweetest Rose of all – my mom.

Thanks, Dad for waiting twenty-five years for Mom.

Contents

Author's Note	v
Dedication	vii
My Mother	ix
Preface	xiii
Always Out There, But Never Known To Me	1
Shtetl Life	3
Passport To Freedom	7
Grojec, Poland	11
Jewish History In Eastern Europe	13
If I Were A Rich Man	17
Brothers and Sisters	29
Grysk, Kriesk, Kraisk?	31
The Diaspora	35

The Name Game	39
The Wedding Photo	45
Home, Sweet Home	49
Coming To America	51
New York Is A Wonderful Town…	57
Random Acts Of Kindness	63
My Dad	69
But We're Cousins…	75
Connecting History	107
Genealogy Without Documentation Is Mythology	113
The Power Of Whitepages.Com	119
A My Name Is Abe	125
Don't Wait Too Long	129
All In The Family	137
Israel Connection	141
Last, But Certainly Not Least	147
Epilogue	159

Preface

Although this is not a historical or reference book, I believe that it is important to have an understanding about some Eastern European history prior to and during the late 19th and early 20th centuries. Hopefully, readers will gain an appreciation for the events that led our ancestors to leave the hardships of their homelands, yet still face the uncertainty of beginning new lives in America.

Throughout the book, I hope to sprinkle stories of lives and incidents which led our Eastern European families, in particular, to leave their loved ones, often travelling alone, bringing with them their memories, traditions, hopes and dreams. I imagine they mostly shared one desire in common – to make a better life for themselves and their families while, most importantly, enjoying personal and religious FREEDOM – the values we hold above all as Americans.

Always Out There, But Never Known To Me

Who were my ancestors? Where did they come from? What were their occupations? Where is my extended family? As I took this wondrous adventure of trying to bring my roots to life, I realized that you can gain strength from your heritage with the knowledge you gather each time you 'meet' another ancestor or family member. WE ARE CUSTODIANS OF OUR FAMILY'S MEMORIES. It is our responsibility to pass along the stories which we discover by means of the genealogical process.

I LOVE being a detective. Perhaps, I missed my true calling. Then again, I may not have appreciated the process years ago. Not having been a jig-saw puzzle fan, I may never have enjoyed the fascination of assembling the pieces and solving the mysteries of my genealogical hunt. When I did become preoccupied with the search for my families, I felt

NOTHING would interfere with the discovery of clues and evidence which would solve my family mystery.

I do, however, want to warn readers that not everyone contacted will have the same exuberance about finding unknown family members. Although disappointing, you must respect their decision. At first, I found it difficult to accept a NO. You are not going to entice everyone or change their minds. Yes, you will have holes in your Family Tree. It's their loss, not yours.

I am fulfilling a dream by leading you through my exploration to find my family members who were always out there but never known to me until I undertook the journey of a lifetime. In the process, I found new family friends and the history of those whom I, unfortunately, will never meet in person. These connections to our family I will pass down to future generations, so that their place in our story will not be lost again or forgotten.

When I embarked upon this genealogical quest in the summer of 2006, I had no idea of the successes that I would amass by 2009. I had an insatiable interest in the historical time period of my ancestors. I know that the next time I see 'Fiddler on The Roof', I will view the story through more personal eyes. Little did I dream that what I believed was a very small ancestral line would become the extended Family Tree which has grown and continues to flourish with each new generation.

Shtetl Life

A shtetl was typically a small city, village or town with a large Jewish community which was located largely in Eastern Europe. Shtetls were primarily found in the 19th century Russian Empire's restricted Pale of Settlement and in the Kingdom of Poland. It was in these villages, now lost to history, that the remarkable culture of the Ashkenazi Jews flourished until its demise during World War II.

Most residents were poor, superstitious and resistant to change. They followed Orthodox Judaism despite outside influence. Their Yiddish language became synonymous with the Ashkenazi Jews of Eastern European shtetls.

Many of our thoughts invariably drift to scenes from "Fiddler on the Roof" as the quintessential story of life in a 19th or early 20th century shtetl. While there was music and dancing, the townspeople were tailors, butchers, fishmongers, shopkeepers, peddlers and dairymen, who worked long, hard days just to sustain their poor lives. Each shtetl was led by a Rabbi who was respected by all Jews in the community.

Shtetls operated on the idea that giving to the needy was not only to be admired, but was essential and expected. The problems of those who needed help were accepted as a responsibility both of the community and of the individual… on earth, the prestige value of good deeds is second only to that of LEARNING. The rewards for benefaction are manifold and are to be reaped both in this life and in the life to come.[1]

As summarized in "Pirkei Avot" by Shimon Hatzaddik's 'three pillars': on three things the world stands. On Torah, on service (of God) and on the acts of human kindness.[2] It is this Tzedaka or charity that remains a key element of Jewish culture.

While wealth was a secondary status, learning and education were the ultimate measures of worth in the shtetl. A hard working person was admired in the community, but he who studied was considered most valuable of all.

My Ruderman ancestors resided in Kraysk or Kraisk – now part of Belarus, then it was in Lithuania. With a mere seven hundred residents, this was certainly one of the smallest of the shtetls recorded in the **First All Russian Census of 1897**. There are few records in existence for Kraisk, none the less, I do hope one day to discover my great grandfather's occupation. I would assume, however, that he may have been a butcher, farmer or dairyman, as my grandfather was a butcher for most of his life in America.

On the other hand, the Bornstein and Hiller families lived in the larger, more thriving community of Gritse, today's Grojec, Poland. Thanks to the stories left by my grandmother, Annie, and grandfather, Sam, I have a clearer picture of the lives they led in Gritse.

Grandma Annie (Chana Yetta) and her mother, Bubba (Grandma)Dina Borensztejn were skilled with a needle and thread. They created beautiful table cloths, towels, and the like. Grandma Annie told stories of how she and her mother had a 'push cart' which they took from town to town, and from which they sold their wares. Grandpa Sam Hiller's brother became an expert leather craftsman, carving saddles and other leather objects.

It was Grandpa Sam, along with Grandma Annie's brother, Abe (Abram) who aspired to become scholars. I know that my grandfather would have loved to become a Rabbi, spending his days debating the aspects of the Torah and the Talmud. When Sam and Abe fled the horrors of the pogroms in Russia and Poland, they knew they would need a skill in order to survive in their newly adopted country. I remember when I was a child how Grandpa Sam continued to visit the Synagogue in Paterson, New Jersey several times per week to pray and study with other immigrants.

> "Gone now are those little towns, where the shoemaker was a poet, the watchmaker a

Elizabeth Ruderman Miller

> philosopher, the barber a troubadour. Gone now are those little towns where the wind joined Biblical songs with Polish tunes and Slavic rue, Where old Jews in orchards in the Shade of cherry trees lamented for the holy walls of Jerusalem. Gone now are those little towns, through the poetic mists, the moons, winds, ponds and the stars above them have recorded in the blood of centuries the tragic tales, the histories of the two saddest nations on earth."
>
> —Antoni Sionimshi,
> "Elegy for the Jewish Villages"

1. Life is With People: The Culture of the Shtetl by Mark Zborowski and Elizabeth Herzog, 1962 edition
2. Excerpt from Pirke Avot (http://www.aish.com/ spirituality/growth/Three_Pillars-Pirke_Avot_12.asfrom aish.com

Passport To Freedom

Words can not express how thrilling it was to discover my Grandfather Sam Hiller's **1908 PASSPORT**. Hidden away between other keepsakes at my Mom's home was this gem encased in a plain black cover. Upon inspection, I was surprised that the writing appeared to be Russian, as my Grandfather Sam always said that the Hiller family was from Poland. It wasn't until I researched further, that I learned about the Russia-Poland connection prior to World War II.

I was anxious to return to California to have my prized possession translated. Fortunately, my rheumatologist has a staff of several women who have themselves immigrated from Russia. During my next appointment, Diana, an assistant, perused the document while I saw the doctor. She was grinning like a Cheshire cat when I returned to the window. She had some wonderful secret she wanted to share with me. Unlike today's passports, she reported, those from one hundred years ago read like pages of someone's biography. As Diana translated the pages, I wrote on yellow post-its, so I could attach the English translation to each page. I do believe that I trembled as I wrote each translation, learning facts about my grandfather which I had never known.

Page one indicated that this was a passport specifically for Jews. It mentioned the city where the passport was issued and the date of March 28, 1908. I learned the exact Yiddish name of my grandfather on the second page Shyje Yacov Giller (there was no letter as in Hiller); was Jewish and was born on June 15, 1882. I was never able to garner the proof of birth for any of my other grandparents. The next few pages read like a little story, adding more important information about my Grandpa Sam. He was living in the Warsawa (Warsaw) Gubernia(province), and he was married to Zhenya Mahlya Dvanra, who was born on January 2, 1885. They were married in 1901 and had a baby daughter, Perla Leya, who died at six month of age.   There was confirmation of Sam's conscription (compulsory service)in the military in 1905, however, it made no mention of his 'inability' to serve.(I knew Grandpa Sam had no military record). I learned that his birth records showed he was from Grojec. The proof of his physical description was literally in black and white with his medium height, black hair and no specific birth marks.

Presenting this information to my aging mother was the kind of gift about which we dream. Mom knew nothing of her half sibling who died at infancy, nor the name of Grandpa's first wife. Even though the passport was in her possession for nearly fifty years, she had never thought to ask anyone about it's contents.

There were two more surprises contained between the pages of this prized possession. The actual **CERTIFICATE OF NATURALIZATION**, although not in pristine condition, was folded in thirds. It was dated June 16, 1915 and stated that my grandfather was thirty-four years old and stood five feet five and one half inches tall. I knew Grandpa Sam until I was in my teens, and I can honestly say that he was taller than my Mom, who was herself that same height. His age and that of my grandmother are correct when compared with his PASSPORT. It is an amazing document!

The second surprise was a clipping from the Paterson, New Jersey Evening News from Monday, May 15, 1950, fifty-nine years to the day on which I am writing this chapter. The Paterson United Jewish Appeal campaign was headed by the 'BACK BONE DIVISION' of the Textile Workers. There, seated, was Grandpa Sam Hiller, and I couldn't have been more proud.

Grojec, Poland

Grojec (Gritse in Yiddish) is a small town in Poland. Jews were permitted, to reside there and were recorded as early as the census in 1754. The Jewish community numbered 1,719 in 1856 (68% of the total population), 3,737 in 1897(61% of the total population) and 4922 in 1921 (56% of the population). On the eve of World War II there were approximately 5,200 Jews living in Grojec.

HOLOCAUST PERIOD

With the entry of the German army on September 8, 1939, terrorization of the Jewish population commenced. On September 12, 1939, all men between the ages of fifteen and fifty-five were forced to assemble at the market, and from there marched on foot to Rawa Mazowiecka, about thirty-seven miles away. Many were shot on the way. During the spring of 1940, about five hundred Jews from

Lodz and the vicinity were forced to settle in Grojec. A ghetto was established in July, 1940, and the plight of the Jewish inhabitants drastically deteriorated. They suffered from hunger, epidemics and the lack of fuel during the winter of 1940-41. About one thousand Jews from nearby locations were brought to the Grojec ghetto that January. On February 23 and 24, 1941, about 2,700 of the Jews in Grojec were deported to the Warsaw Ghetto, where they shared the fate of Warsaw Jewry. The Grojec ghetto was liquidated in September, 1942. About 3000 surviving Jewish inmates were deported to Bialobrzegi (a small town on the Warsaw-Radom highway), and from there were all sent to the Treblinka death camp. In Grojec itself, only three hundred Jews remained, 83 of whom were deported after some time to a slave labor camp in Russia near Smolensk, where almost all were murdered. The last two hundred Jews were executed in the summer of 1943 in a forest near Gora Kalwaria. After the war, the Jewish community in Grojec was not reconstituted. Organizations of former Jewish residents of Grojec were established in Israel, France, the U.S., Canada and Argentina.

Only one of my mother's cousins survived the death camps during the Holocaust. After the liberation of Buchenwald, seventeen year old Benjamin Hiller came to the United States to his uncle, my grandfather, Samuel Hiller.

Jewish History In Eastern Europe

The Diaspora (the presence of Jews outside of the Land of ancient Israel) transplanted Jewish exiles to Babylonia, Spain, the Mediterranean and the Middle East. Another thousand years would pass before Jews would establish a foothold in Europe where, in about 900 A.D. we can trace the beginnings of the Yiddish and the Jewish culture. In Central Europe, Jews were limited to trades such as that of merchants engaged in long-distance travel. During the Middle Ages as Jews moved to new areas in France and Germany, they built flourishing centers for Sephardim. As the communities of Central Europe grew, Jews developed a hybrid language of their own, combining German, Hebrew and Aramaic. This local vernacular, **Yiddish**, would unite the secular and the religious into the Jewish culture that would define Ashkenazai life in Eastern Europe until the Holocaust.

Elizabeth Ruderman Miller

Jews who lived in the German lands suffered continual injustices from the Crusades, the Plague (for which Jews were often blamed and held responsible for its devastation) to finally being expelled and driven East toward the newly forming Kingdoms of Lithuania and Poland. Jews from the West brought many traditions with them, including worship in synagogues, burial societies, religious schools for children and governing bodies. Hebrew continued to be the religious language while Yiddish remained a significant and distinguishing aspect of Eastern European Jewish life and culture.

The cradle of Ashkenazi culture in Jewish Poland overshadowed that in the German lands. Notably, during the Middle Ages, Jews from the West travelled East to study and conduct business in the commercial center of towns such as Vilna, Brest and Cracow. Jewish-centered communities increased during the 18th and 19th centuries, enabling Jews more occupations opportunities in the trades, crafts and land leasing for nobles. The three basic types of Jewish communities, the city (shtot), small Jewish urban settlements (shtets) and the tiny scattered communities (yishuv) meshed nicely into the Jewish world of the day.

Jewish communities have been found in the Rhine valley since ancient Roman times. German Jews suffered from extreme violence during the Middle Ages causing the migration to the Slavic and Baltic regions of Europe. The language which they carried with them was the roots of

Yiddish. **If your ancestors were Eastern European Jews in 1490, THEIR ancestors probably lived in Germany in 1000 C.E.**

The Sephardic Jews in 1492 - Spanish Jews immigrated to Portugal after they were ordered to convert or be expelled. The Ladino language arose as a result of Jews bringing their language with them to the Balkans and the Middle East. Many of the Jews who left Portugal settled in the Netherlands. **If your ancestors were Dutch or New York Jews then, there is a good possibility that they lived in Spain or Portugal in 1490.**

Polish nobles employed Jewish overseers to Administer to their lands in the combined Kingdoms of Lithuania and Poland. **If your ancestors were Ukranian Jews in 1800 C.E., their ancestors most probably lived in Poland and Lithuania in 14 C.E.**

Jews from Central Europe first settled in Lithuania during the last half of the 14th century. Anyone who lived under the Lithuanian rule during the 16th and 17th centuries in the areas including Poland, Minsk and Belarus were referred to as **Litvaks.** During the 19th century, Litvaks moved further into what is today's Poland, especially the area of Lodz where the famous textile industry began. Jews have appeared in Lithuanian census lists as early as the 17th century.

If I Were A Rich Man

In 19th century Russia/Poland, in the small shtetl of Gritse(Greetz'a) (n Yiddish), (Grojec in Polish), Schyje (she'ya) Yacov Giler(Hiller) was born to Leonard Joseph and his wife (unknown name) on June 15, 1882. Schyje grew to become a scholar, a learned man which was a very common calling during this time period in Eastern Europe. He may have possibly become a Rabbi, but Schyje had the misfortune of being drafted into the military sometime in 1905. He was considered of medium height and build, with no poor health history and there was no reason why he would not have to obey his call to duty. **ALL OF THIS INFORMATION WAS VERIFIED IN HIS PRECIOUS PASSPORT.**

Not wanting to serve for moral and spiritual reasons, Schyje became a desperate man. He went on a 'diet' of vinegar and water with the intent of losing enough weight that he would be considered physically and medically unsuitable to report for duty. He succeeded! Perhaps even on the brink of death, he suffered from extremely poor health for some time, however, thankfully, he did recover from this brave ordeal.

Like a dream come true, on December 31, 1908 Schyje, age twenty-six finally sailed on the SS Main out of Bremen, Germany arriving at Ellis Island on January 12, 1909. His companion on this journey was twenty-one year old Abram Borensztejn, a good friend from their hometown of Gritse. The discovery of the **Ship's Manifest** on **ANCESTRY.COM** was an amazing experience. Not only did I discover the correct spelling of my grandfather's Yiddish name, but the **manifest included his wife's name** as well (I could not make out her given name until his passport was translated.) I was able to inform my new cousins, Abe Bornstein's grandchildren about their grandmother who was also left behind in Poland. They were poor young scholars who sought a better life in America, and with the promise of learning a new trade (from former town dwellers who had already emigrated), their destination became Paterson, New Jersey, well known for its silk industry. Many men from Gritse had made the long journey across the Atlantic to Paterson, most leaving behind their families, but with thoughts of bringing them to America when they became established. Schyje and Abram did just that – leaving behind their wives and children. It must have been a lonely time for them in their new homes, but they would never again be threatened with the fear of conscription (compulsory enrollment for service in a country's armed forces) or from the terror of the European **Pogroms** ever again.

POGROMS

As far back as the Maccabean Revolt in 167 BCE, following the conquests of Alexander the Great, there has been anti-Semitic violence. During the height of ancient Roman occupation, Jews refused to accept Roman rule over Palestine inciting the outbreak of numerous riots against them. The first officially recorded pogroms against the Jews dates back to the Crusades in France and Germany followed by the annihilation of London Jews from 1189-1190. Although Jews prospered in Spain, under Islamic controlled Spain, there were Pogroms against the Jews between the 11th through the 15th centuries, notably the 1066 Granada massacre where thousands of Jews were killed. Possibly the most notorious Pogrom happened when, in 1465, Muslim mobs murdered all but 11 Jews in Fez.

During the years of the European Plague, the numbers of Jews who succumbed to the illness most probably did not reach the numbers who were murdered because of the fear that they were somehow responsible for the outbreak and spread of the Plague. Of importance are the Jews who survived during those dark days, and who fled to Poland, where the government allowed them to seek refuge when other countries refused. This small group of surviving Jews may actually be responsible for the repopulation of Jews around the world.

The series of large scale, violent armed mob attacks on the Jews in Russia in the late 19th and early 20th centuries became known as POGROMS(po'grom) or riots against people and property of a religious or national minority. False rumors circulated associating the Jews with the assassination of Czar Alexander II in 1881. Violence erupted. Mobs attacked with intoxicated hatred against the Jews in more than two hundred shtetls and cities. With the anti-Semitic policies of the Russian government between 1881 – 1917, the pogroms escalated. This led to the first wave of emigration by Russian Jews to the United States.

There were anti-Jewish riots in Odessa in the mid-19th century. A very bloody surge of pogroms took place between 1903-1906. The most serious of these pogroms was in 1905 against the Odessa Jews during which historians recorded more than 2500 Jewish deaths.

After the publication of the Czar's Manifesto in 1905, pogroms escalated to over six hundred towns in the area of the Pale of Settlement. During the Russian Revolution of 1917, atrocities against Jews were responsible for the murder of up to a quarter of a million leaving hundreds of thousands of Jewish orphans.

In more modern times, pogroms were incited by the Nazis, especially during the early days of World War II. Kristallnacht, the 'Night of Broken Glass' describes the nights when shattered Jewish store windowpanes blanketed the German streets. During the nights of November 9 and 10, Nazi youth prowled through Jewish neighborhoods, broke windows of almost 7,500 Jewish businesses and burned all 101 synagogues. Over 25,000 Jews were arrested and sent to concentration camps.[3] As a result of the 'spontaneous outbursts', Hitler ordered the coordinated effort for solving the 'Jewish question' – the elimination of all Jews from the German economy. Many believe Kristallnacht to be the turning point in German policy regarding the Jews and possibly the beginning of what we now call the Holocaust – the path to the Jewish 'Final Solution.'

The brutal cruelty against Jews over the millennium sent Jews on their paths of emigration to other parts of the world for their survival. Jewish settlements have been found flourishing in China, South America, and South Africa to name just a few locations.

After some time, both Schyje and Abram supposedly divorced their first wives. I say 'supposedly' because I have no official documentation to verify this claim. My assumption is that Schyje's first marriage may have been 'arranged' which was the custom in many countries at that time. As a young man in Gritse, Schyje had really fallen in love with Abram's sister, Chana Yetta Borensztejn who some time after her brother's arrival in America became a widow with a young son and daughter. Schyje, now Samuel Jacob Hiller had his good friend, Abram, now Abe Bornstein write to Chana asking for her hand in marriage if she would make the journey to Paterson. After agreeing, Chana Yetta sailed aboard the ship, the Lapland, from Antwerp, Belgium on August 20, 1912 arriving at Ellis Island on September 2, 1912.

I wanted to view the proof! The first extraordinary discovery I had was finding the confirmation of Grandma Annie's voyage to America. After signing up for **ELLISISLAND.ORG** and choosing my password, I typed in the surname Hiller. To this day, no one in our family knows the last name of Grandma Annie's first husband. Taking a chance that she might use the surname of her husband-to-be, that became my choice. There were many Hillers listed, but none under the name of Chana Yetta. Before using her Americanized first name, I wanted to be certain that I had the proper translation.

I had been informed that **JEWISHGEN.ORG** had a section titled **SEARCH THE GIVEN NAMES DATA BASES(GNDBs)**. It allows you to use either of two different search directions: European-to-Foreign names or Foreign-to-European names. I chose the former and typed in the European country: Poland, the name search: Chana, the search field: Hebrew+Yiddish+EuroSecular, Search type: Global(Plain text), and the foreign country: United States.

Within seconds I was viewing **The Polish Given Names Database.** The very first of twenty-six hits contained these details:

How Will I Know Where I'm Going, If I Don't Know Where I've Been?

LEGAL/HEBREW:	CHANA/ANNA/ANNI
YIDDISH:	ANNA/ANNE/ANNI
US NAME:	ANNA, ETC

This was one of the times that I worked late into the night not wanting to sleep until I found my Grandmother's **SHIP'S MANIFEST**. My reward came about midnight; **passenger number 63 was Anni Hiller** whose **residence was Gritse. She arrived in 1912 at the age of 21.** With a three hour time difference, I almost couldn't wait the six hours until I could phone my Mom and read her the long awaited news.

Sam and Annie were married, but the exact date of their wedding is unknown. No record of their marriage has been found yet I do have a black and white copy of a picture taken on their supposed wedding day.

The couple welcomed a daughter, Rose, my Mom, on October 29, 1913. At her advanced age, it isn't surprising that Mom's recollection of dates was slightly confused, but now I was fortunate to have the documents to share with her and the rest of the family. I am also blessed that my Mom and her parents had a wonderful relationship and they shared detailed stories about the family with her.

With connections from Gritse, Grandpa Sam was trained as a weaver in one of the silk factories in Paterson. Grandma was a stay-at-home housewife and mother. Both prayed that World War I would end quickly, and they could send for their children still residing in Poland. Fortunately, all of the children lived with close family and friends in Gritse while awaiting money for their passage so they could reunite with their parent and new sister.

Upon his arrival in United States in 1909, Sam Hiller was taken under the wings of his **LANDSMEN** (fellow Jews who came from the same town or district, especially in Eastern Europe, from Gritse). He toiled in the silk manufacturing industry in Paterson, New Jersey. All of the raw silk was imported, much of it coming from China. There were four stages of silk fabric production: THROWING – the twisting of the silk fibers into threads which could be used on the looms; DYEING; WEAVING and FINISHING. Immigrants, many of whom came from Poland or Germany, England or Italy worked in the silk factories. There were no child labor laws at the time, so a child might begin working about the age of 14 or 15 and spend the rest of his life working in silk manufacturing or the factories.

January through May of 1913 hit the silk industry with hard times. Eight hundred silk weavers walked off the job stating their grievance on the four-loom system, which enabled a single weaver to handle four looms. This action would eliminate what could amount to one out of every two jobs. The ribbon weavers soon joined forces with the weavers and then with the dye house workers. The workers talked about unionizing; the mill owners refused to give in to demands. Workers and their families stood firmly together, but families were on the verge of starvation, and owners were beginning to farm out mill work to factories in Pennsylvania. Although the owners never gave in to workers demands, they lost millions of dollars in profits. The strike committee voted to settle with individual mills and the two-loom system remained the standard in Paterson until 1919. The decline of the Paterson silk industry came with the introduction of Rayon, the artificial silk.

Sam Hiller was a rare example of a man who rose from the ranks of the weavers to become an independent manufacturer. He saved enough money to buy first one loom and then a second, renting space in one of the many factories in Paterson. His business was called REGENT SILK MILLS, INC. During the dismal days during World War I, the silk industry certainly suffered. My Mom remembered that my grandfather would bring home bolts of newly woven silk fabric and attach the rolls to nails that were driven into the top rail of a chair. Grandma Annie would then painstakingly inspect each section of the fabric picking out small threads that did not belong on the exquisite material. This was the job of the FINNISHERS, so if Annie was able to perform the task at home, Sam would have one less worker to hire.

It must also be noted that in order to bring additional money into the home during the war days, Annie would prepare lunch for Sam's factory workers. They would pay her twenty-five cents for lunch which helped support their little family.

After the silk workers' strike in 1913, Paterson's share of the national silk production continued to dip. Sam had been communicating with other manufacturers who had left the city and set up business in Pennsylvania. He heard that there was a need for a new silk factory in Port Jervis, New York – just across the Delaware River from Pennsylvania.

In the early 1930s, he took his family and his looms transporting them the less than one hundred miles to the small city of Port Jervis, where his new factory was named HILLERSON SILK MILLS, INC. It was located on the River Road overlooking the banks of the Delaware, a truly picturesque location for any business with its tree line view of the river. My Mom was twenty years old and served as Grandpa Sam's bookkeeper. Until her death, at age 95, she continued to keep her own set of accounting books.

About the time that Hillerson Silk Mills, Inc. opened it's doors, Rose met the man who would become my father, Henry Ruderman. Had her father not made the decision to move to Port Jervis, Rose would never have met Henry.

When Rose needed a dress for the wedding, Grandpa Sam used his 'connections' in the silk industry to trade services for the satin used to make Mom's gown. The material chosen for her gown was also used to make beautiful undergarments of the day. The 1938 cost for sewing this creation was $2.98!

There never was a 'rich man', as Grandpa Sam suffered bankruptcy not once, but twice.

3   Snyder, LouisL Encyclopedia of the Third Reich. New York: Paragon House, 1989:201

Brothers and Sisters

It would be another seven years before the Hiller and Bornstein families would be reunited at Ellis Island. With peace restored after World War I and enough funds secured for their passages, two members of the Hiller family and five from the Bornstein family set sail on the SS Rotterdam departing from the port of Rotterdam, The Netherlands on July 3, 1920. Their voyage concluded nine days later when they arrived at Ellis Island to the waiting arms of their loved ones.

The first list I located was entitled, **LIST OR MANIFEST OF ALIEN PASSENGERS OF THE UNITED STATES.** I had only been researching a short time, and the description and page configuration was unfamiliar to me. I didn't realize, at first what was staring back at me. Upon further inspection, and by increasing the magnification to 150%, I printed a copy of the **SHIP'S DOCUMENT** and sat transfixed in wonder at the page I was reading.

Elizabeth Ruderman Miller

My Mom had never mentioned the Yiddish names of her half siblings who were born in Poland. My best clue was the **entry on line #2: HILLER, RANA, age 40, female, passage paid by her BROTHER.** The notes added that Rana was going to SAM HILLER, 213 Graham Avenue, Paterson, New Jersey! Rana's former place of residence: GROJEC! I immediately phoned my Mom, who confirmed the aforementioned address as her childhood residence. More importantly, Rana was Grandpa Sam's sister who had served as the guardian of Sam's son during his absence from Poland. My sister, Rona was named for Rana, who was known as Tante Fanny to the family. It all made sense as to how Mom and Dad arrived at my sister's name selection. Travelling with Rana was a 15 year old boy, Nusson, noted as having RED HAIR and who was coming to his father, Sam Hiller. On the **SHIP'S MANIFEST** with which I was familiar, there were never identification notes, however, the **ALIEN LISTS** contained descriptions of passenger's traits which were noted for identification. During my childhood, I remember that my Uncle Nathan had red hair, and only recently, did his son, Herb mentioned that his nickname was 'Red' when Nathan was a kid. **THE IMPORTANCE OF DOCUMENTATION AND VERBAL CONFIRMATION FROM FAMILY IS THE BEST KNOWLEDGE OF ALL**.

Grysk, Kriesk, Kraisk?

GOOGLE is a wonderful tool, but doesn't do the trick all of the time. In the case of trying to find my paternal grandparents' shtetl (the Russian village in which they had lived), I couldn't find anything resembling the spelling Grysk, which appeared on my Grandfather Morris Ruderman's DECLARATION OF INTENTION FOR IMMIGRATION. Trying **JEWISHGEN.ORG,** I was able to conduct a *SEARCH FOR A SURNAME* OR *SEARCH FOR A TOWN.* I revisited the **JEWISHGEN.ORG** website countless times during my three year search. For Jewish genealogical research, it is invaluable.

Grysk turned out to be KRAYSK, which was the spelling of the tiny shtetl (village) formerly in the Uyzed (district) of Vileika in the Gubernia (province) of Vilna which in the days of the 19th century was part of Lithuania. Prior to 1842, the Vileika District belonged to the Minsk Gubernia. Since World War I, the spelling of the village is primarily seen as

KRAISK, and now is part of the province of Byelorussia in what is now Belarus.

I began with the understanding that the Ruderman family lived near Minsk. KRAISK is much closer to the city of Vilna/Vilnius, which had a thriving Jewish community, and was often known as 'the Venice of Eastern Europe'. At the first all-Russian census of 1897, Kraysk had a population of under 700, with slightly over 500 Jews. Joel Ratner, Vilna District Research Coordinator for **JEWISHGEN.ORG** answered my email with a statistical analysis of all towns in the Vileika Districk with a population in excess of 500 person for year. The book from which this extract was taken was originally published in French, and the shtetl appeared as BOURGADE KRAISK.

January 2008 was the month in which I would contact a Russian man who would provide many answers about our family's little shtetl of Kraisk. After discovering the **JEWISH HERITAGE RESEARCH GROUP** of Belarus online, I began corresponding with its director, Yuri Dorn. His email, dated January 20, 2008 thanked me for making the contact and explained that his organization was, indeed, familiar with Kraisk. Just months before my first note, the local authorities of Kraisk built a new road through the town. Unfortunately, the road was too close to the old Jewish cemetery, which was located on a hill. After completing the road construction, the cemetery began to slide down the hill. Yuri added, "One person who merely drove by noticed this and called us. We went there right away to investigate the situation. What we saw was a gravestone already laying on the road. We counted 48 tombstones in that cemetery."

This disturbing news was intensified after a response from a considerate Russian woman named Tatiana, whose grandmother appears to be the only Jew residing in Kraisk. Tatiana forwarded three pictures of the Kraisk cemetery, including that of an exposed human skull in desperate need of reburying.

It was obvious that this was one of the hundreds or thousands of Jewish cemeteries which were in desperate need of repair. Yuri noted that the majority of Jewish records for Kraisk are prior to 1858 and that there were only random records after that date, among which are: a revision(census list) from 1874 and 1886; a list of male conscripts (draftees) during 1862-1889; a list of tax papers from the latter part of the 19th century and some foreign passport applications from 1898-1905. It was during the years when the Russian Czar allowed Jews in the country. Later, in 1836 Jews were allowed to purchase land. According to census records, the population consisted of 100% Jews at that time. The main occupation of Jews of Kraisk was agricultural rural settlement which was part Of the Vilna Gubernia. Unfortunately, there are no formal records to tell the history of this shtetl.

Returning to **JEWISHGEN.ORG** and performing a town search for the shtetl, Kraisk in Belarus, I retrieved six researchers who were interested in the same community. This didn't appeared very promising. Six researchers represented only ten surnames, none of which were my last name of Ruderman or Cohen. I emailed each one of them and received a note from all but one. Low and behold, the person who was looking for a Ruderman in Port Jervis, New York also appeared on this list from Kraysk, looking for the surname, KASDIN, which was unfamiliar to me.

The Diaspora

The presence of Jews outside of the ancient land of Israel, the Jewish Diaspora, was a result of the expulsion or emigration of Jews from Israel. It commenced during the $8^{th} - 6^{th}$ centuries B.C, when the ancient Jewish kingdom was conquered, the first Temple of Solomon was destroyed and the Jewish people were expelled from the land. This was later followed by the siege of Jerusalem by the Romans, and their occupation of Judea in the 1st and 2nd Centuries A.D. In 70 A.D. the Romans demolished the second Temple which had been reconstructed in 516 B.C. and renovated by Herod the Great in 20 B.C. For several centuries afterward, a number of Jewish communities were established in the Middle East. However, the defeat of the Jewish revolt by the Roman Empire, their losing control of Judah and the knowledge that Jews were sold into slavery, contributed to the scattering of millions of Jews throughout the vast Roman Empire of the 1st century A.D.

Jews were deported from the Kingdom of Israel beginning thousand of years ago when the Assyrians conquered the land. Persian Jews have lived in the current territories of Iran for almost 3000 years.

Josephus, the well-known Jewish historian, noted that the lands of Israel, Babylonia and Syria had the largest Jewish population. Egypt's Jewish inhabitants may have numbered as high as one million, nearly one-eighth of it's population with Alexandria the most important of the Egyptian cities. At this time, at the height of Rome's territorial dominance, the Roman government sent its legions to Judea to capture Jerusalem and destroy the heart of the religious and national life of the Jews – the TEMPLE. It was the goal of the Romans to totally destroy Jerusalem and prevent the regeneration of the Jewish nation. SOUND FAMILIAR? Both Emperors Trajan and Hadrian were responsible for killing vast number of Jews during their reign. Jerusalem became a Roman colony; its citizens were instructed to worship the pagan Roman gods. Jews were even forbidden entrance into the city for a time. Fortunately, there were small numbers of Jewish communities in Palestine, the Negev, Jordan and the Galilee. During this destructive period, Jews were often sold as slaves or transported as captives. With the forced expulsions, the Diaspora grew, and Jews were sent to various Roman provinces in North Africa, Europe and the Middle East.

How Will I Know Where I'm Going, If I Don't Know Where I've Been?

It is important to remember that it was during the Middle Ages that Jews divided into two very distinctive groups: the ASHKENAZI comprised of Northern and Eastern European Jews and the SEPHARDIC including Spanish and Middle Eastern Jews. Ashkenazi and Sephardic Jews shared the horrors of persecution and forced expulsion, and their descendants ultimately joined to fight for the State of Israel after World War II.

The Name Game

I never knew the grandmother in whose honor I was named. Sarah Cohen Ruderman, whose Yiddish name was Eske, Esther, became know as Sarah upon her arrival in America. I secured indisputable confirmation of her name association when I used the **JEWISHGEN.ORG Belarus Given Names Database,** searching for the name **Sarah** and happily found that the Yiddish origins and Yiddish nickname is, in fact, **ESKE/ESKA/ESHKE/ESHKA**! Sarah died from complications of Pemphagus, an insidious, blistering, autoimmune disorder of the skin just two weeks before my birth. Learning the details of my grandmother's medical history became very important when I was diagnosed with the rare autoimmune disorder, Erythromelalgia. Although I will never be able to verify the connection, it is likely that autoimmune disorders are genetic, particularly between close female relatives.

Typically, Sarah was a short, Eastern European woman whose pictures(there are only two in existence), depict a much older woman than her chronological age. Her **immigration records** have eluded me, but I will continue searching the multitude of COHENs and the variants until I have exhausted the files.

My knowledge of the Ruderman family was so limited. The meaning and origin of my surname as it appears in **ANCESTRY.COM's, The Ruderman Name in History,** which is part of the Generations Network, states that Ruderman was 1. Jewish (Ashkenazic): metonymic, which is a figure of speech using a word or phrase as a substitute for one which is closely substituted (i.e., using The White House for the President) or an occupational name from the German *'Ruder', 'oar'* plus Mann *'man'* or 2. German: from *Ruder* (pet form of the Germanic personal name Rothari formed with *hrod* 'renown') plus 'man'. Importantly, is the description from **Alexander Beider, noted authority on the History of Russian Surnames**, that Ruderman was common in *Vileijka*, the area of Vilna near which my Ruderman ancestors lived during the 19th Century.

My Ruderman family was from 'near Minsk' was the extent of my information prior to 2006. It was my belief that the surname Ruderman was very uncommon. Little did I know that when I **Googled** the name, there would be many Ruderman listings - but were any of them MY family? I found the name Ruderman on **Jewishgen.Org**.

and attempted to find shtetls or small Russian towns in which the name appeared. There were three major areas now located in Belarus, but originally in Vilna prior to 1917 – Dolginovo, Samolkovichi and Radoshkovichi. It would, however, be months later, when I made my first connection with a cousin, that I would identify my Ruderman family's home town.

With the death of each of my grandparents, my mother and father were given simple black memorial books from the synagogues – each was inscribed with their date of death, their Hebrew names and room for signatures of relatives and friends who attended the burial ceremony. Traditionally, females were named 'the daughter of' (i.e. Eske Dina bat or bas Dovid), and males received names with 'the son of' Jacob ben Moshe)for their Hebrew names. It was only in the late 18th and early 19th centuries when you could find common surnames on headstones in Jewish cemeteries.

GIVEN NAMES

There was an old Jewish superstition which maintained that naming a child after a LIVING relative was 'bad luck'- that the angel of death, who was an easily confused spirit, might take a baby by mistake when coming for an older relative. Most of us do not believe in such beliefs any longer, however a universal view is that a man shows arrogance if he names a child after himself (i.e. Jr., II, III). There are rare occasions when we find a Jewish male child named after his father.

It became more common over the centuries for Jews living in very Gentile countries or lands to take local names to eliminate being ostracized in business and with the government. Rabbis, seeing this trend and fearing that the practice of Hebrew naming might become extinct, found it necessary to issue a religious ruling (takkaah), requiring all Jews to have a Hebrew name. Now, as then, Hebrew names are used for religious rituals such as the reciting of a blessing from the Torah reading (aliyah), for a marriage contract (ketubah), for a Jewish headstone, in ceremonies, when prayers are said for the ill during a Friday night or Saturday morning service and during prayers said for the deceased (yizkor). During modern times, there is no set rule that your Hebrew given name must correspond with your secular name or visa versa (i.e. Jeffrey is your given name; Moshe could still be your Hebrew name).

SURNAMES

Prior to the 18th and 19th centuries, Jews' surnames were personal and taken from their fathers. A female named Chana born to David would have been Chana bat or bas (the daughter of) Dovid. However, when Chana married Moshe, and their son Boruch was born, his Hebrew name would be Boruch ben (son of) Moshe. These names were one generational.

Jews lived with autonomy until the European governments subjected them to the same state bureaucratic record keeping as all Gentile citizens. This occurred in Czarist Russia in the early 1800s and in Poland and German in the final quarter of the 1700s. Jewish names were primarily of German, Yiddish, Hebrew, Polish, Russian and Byelrussian origin. The history of surnames contains evidence of war and territorial disputes between Poland and Russia. These influenced Jewish migration and the process of community formation.

There were several ways in which Jews selected 'new' surnames: a Jew may have chosen a surname because he liked the name of the European city in which he lived. Those were translated 'resident of' as in Minsk-Y or Berlin-ER. Often, with the movement of the Jews during the centuries, a Jew may like the name of the new city in which you now resided. The practice of CLASSIFYING people by professions was popular during the Diaspora. When this took place, the name followed the descendants even if future family members did not continue to work in that field. One of the emerging trades was that of the tailor. Several names which arose from this occupation were Portnoy(Russian for tailor), Hait (Yiddish for tailor), Kravetz (Russian for tailor). Other names indicated the specialization in a trade such as Scher (scissors), Nodl (needle) or Press (iron).

It is often impossible to trace modern surnames back to the twelve Jewish tribes of Israel or other Jewish

Biblical background. However, the surname COHEN is incontrovertibly of Hebrew origin. Cohen is associated with the tribe of Aaron which has come to mean Priest. Similarily, LEVI/LEVY is connected with the tribe linked to Jacob. These people were considered to be the Priests' assistants. If you have a recent ancestor who became a Rabbi, it is probable that the family were COHEN, members of the priestly tribe.

The Wedding Photo

My parents, Rose Hiller and Henry Ruderman 'kept company' for five years before becoming engaged and setting a wedding date. It was during the height of the Depression, and for many young couples, the thought of planning a wedding reception for almost one hundred people was out of the question. Grandpa Sam had taken out an insurance policy worth five hundred dollars. It matured at just the perfect time for the happy couple. Grandpa Morris Ruderman was anxious for his sister, Esther Ruderman Kasden, who was living in the upstate New York city of Rochester, to attend the wedding of his only son. Perhaps the underlying reason that our families never knew each other was that Esther did NOT attend the wedding after all.

The handsome black and white, panoramic photo from their October 30, 1938 nuptials was the catalyst which propelled me into a daily, three year quest of my genealogical heritage. Knowing that it contained photographic proof of family members, I had the picture copied so that I would be able to send it, along with duplicates of my contemporary family to all newly found relatives.

Remarkably saved along with this treasured piece of history, was a little wooden box which had gone unnoticed for over fifty years. When I opened the little leather box, it contained the detailed plans for my parents' reception, table by table. Under the carefully folded pages, which were actually ledger sheets from my Grandfather Sam Hiller's silk mill in Port Jervis, were tiny 3 X 1 inch reply cards noting the guests who would be attending the autumn wedding in Manhattan. The papers were just shy of seventy years old and were in mint condition – even my mother's scripted handwriting, which was in pencil, was perfectly legible.

Fortunately, all female members of both sides of our immediate family were wearing corsages, making them instantly recognizable. Eventually, ALL of the women and girls in attendance were identified. There were, however, ninety-four guests in attendance, many of whom were extended family who needed to named. Knowing that I had only two living relatives who appeared in the wedding picture, I immediately mailed a copy to my first cousin, Edie, who was about thirteen years old at the time of the photograph. My Mom, the only other person of record had one of the original copies to peruse.

TALK WITH YOUR AGING RELATIVES. THEY ARE ESSENTIAL IN GATHERING ACCURATE

How Will I Know Where I'm Going, If I Don't Know Where I've Been?

INFORMATION AND MAKING CORRECT IDENTIFICATION. DON'T WAIT TOO LONG. THEIR MEMORIES FADE, AND YOU, LIKE I, MAY ONLY HAVE LIMITED RESOURCES UPON WHICH TO CALL.

Edie, my Dad's niece and my closest cousin, was able to recognize on of the original family immigrants – my Uncle Jacob Cohen, Jack after his arrival. Jack was Grandma Sarah Cohen Ruderman's younger brother, who immigrated with his sister in 1898. As of this writing, I have yet to verify their actual immigration records, but intend to continue the search until their discovery. Edie also noted other Cohen cousins, long since deceased, but whose census records may be available with the release of the 1940 census in 2012.

Of the ninety-four wedding guests, there were three young teenage women. As luck would have it, Edie recognized the other two as Blossom and Sylvia Wasserman. They were the grandchildren of the third Cohen sibling who emigrated to the United States – Ceclia Cohen Kahn, older sister of Sarah and Jack. Ceclia and Herman Kahn's only child, Dorothy had married Jacob/Jack Wasserman, and Blossom and Sylvia were their daughters.

I knew absolutely nothing about the Cohen side of my family, but began with searching the records of **ANCESTRY.COM** to find proof of their existence.

Home, Sweet Home

As part of the Minisink Valley, Port Jervis, New York, just under 10,000 residents, is located where the Delaware and Neversink rivers meet at the junction of New York, New Jersey and Pennsylvania between the Catskills and Pocono Mountains. The vistas are beautiful during the Spring when the views of the mountains are abundant with the soft colors of the budding trees. The landscape is breathtaking after the crisp nights coax the leaves to change to their golden colors in the Fall. This part of the state is dotted with small towns, hamlets and 'villes' far smaller than even Port Jervis. It is a short ride across the Mid-Delaware bridge to Matamoras, Pennsylvania. The Tri-States bridge connects Port Jervis with Montague, New Jersey. The Minisink Valley was the setting of many Indian raids during the Revolutionary War days and is home to the Fort Decker, along the Delaware River famous for being visited by George Washington during the Revolutionary War. During the 1880s, rafts made their way down the swollen waters of the Delaware carrying lumber. For decades since, the recreational rafting industry has flourished during the sultry, summer days.

'MADE IN PORT JERVIS'

Since it became incorporated as a village in 1853, Port Jervis had been a transportation center as a stop on the Delaware and Hudson Canal (D&H) and the New York and Lake Erie Railroad. Because of this distinction, many industries saw Port Jervis as a favorable spot for factory development. Products from these companies have been seen around the country and the world. Factories were in abundance producing goods such as candy, dress gloves, shoes, coats, sweaters, solar panels, soda bottling, wallpaper print, ice cream and silk "as was the case" with my own family's Hillerson Silk Mill on the River Road in the 1930s. The city is proud to continue its history of manufacturing with products such as glass (which has been made in Port Jervis since 1912), cosmetics, pharmaceuticals, office and stationery supplies (including the world's first biodegradable pen!) and custom-designed modular homes.

Port Jervis, New York was listed as one of America's 10 Coolest Small Towns with fewer than 10,000 residents on the 2008 Yahoo Travel site.

Coming To America

At best, all I knew about my Ruderman ancestors was that they came from somewhere near Minsk. In 2006, well before their television commercials, I joined **ANCESTRY.COM** and **JEWISHGEN.ORG.** I hoped to learn as much about the Ruderman immigrants as I could.

My search began trying to locate two important Documents - 1. **Census records** for Morris Ruderman and his family - 2. **Naturalization documents** proving Grandpa Morris' immigration information. After assuming, incorrectly, that Haven, Dad's birthplace was located in Orange County, as is Port Jervis, I called information for the **Sullivan County (NY) Clerk's Office** to confirm that I was looking in the right office. The clerk was very polite and took down the specific information which I had about my grandfather. It's my feeling that dealing with a small town community, such as Monticello, New York, offers a more personal touch, and for that, I was grateful. Thanks to a suggestion by **Gladys Paulin, Editor of OnBoard, The Newsletter of the Board for Certification of Genealogists,** I knew to ask for the entire file including the Petition (the final papers). A copy of the entire file is available through the FREEDOM OF INFORMATION ACT request.

A particularly important letter arrived on May 4, 2007. **"Enclosed please find a copy of the Declaration of Intention that I found for Morris Ruderman. It was the only thing I could find."** It was signed by a Sullivan County clerk. I was actually looking at a copy of the form which my grandfather had completed on February 8, 1916. It stated my grandfather was a butcher by that time, but the additional details were absolutely fascinating, if not completely factual. Grandpa Morris wrote that he was born in GRYSK, VILNA, RUSSIA. After searching for village names and finding nothing spelled GRYSK, I emailed and spoke with other researchers, who agreed that this must be KRAISK. Translating his hometown into an English spelling often produced unusual spelling. This conclusion was enormous both in finding the Ruderman birth shtetl and confirming the relationship of his siblings.

My guess is that he left Kovno by rail to a seaport. It is known that many immigrants did not correctly remember their year of arrival or even the correct port. It was easy to say New York, especially when that was their final destination. Boston passengers to New York frequently were put aboard small coastal vessels and taken to New York after their arrival.

Additionally, Kovno or Kaunas was not a port of departure. People from there most likely sailed from German, Latvian or Scandinavian ports, usually Bremen or Hamburg. This advice was also imparted by Gladys Paulin.

Most doubtable was his statement that he sailed on the BULGARIA arriving at Ellis Island on April 20, 1900. Checking in the **MORTON ALLAN DICECTORY OF EUROPEAN STEAMSHIP ARRIVALS,** the Bulgaria did NOT sail during this particular time. There was, however, a BELGRAVIA, which docked at Ellis Island on that date. Unfortunately, the name Moshe Ruderman or similar variants does not appear on the **SHIP'S MANIFEST.** My grandfather told my Mom and Dad that he had been drafted into the Russian army, and that he 'escaped.' Others have agreed that it is possible that he secured a passport and entered the United States under an assumed name. Although intriguing, this senario has, frustratingly, not helped me find the immigrations records for Morris Ruderman.

Written in handwriting lengthwise on the paper was a note stating "A certified copy issued on May 1, 1922, pursuant to letter dated April 20, 1922. File No. 2333-d-295 signed with the stamp of J. Maxwell Knapp, clerk. Even **NARA** (the National Archives) in Washington D.C. had no idea what this meant, and had no documentation in their records.

Although disappointed, I had to accept, at least for the time being, there was no further information I could find for my grandfather. It is possible that with his limited education, Grandpa Morris never filed the next set of papers, the **PETITION FOR NATURALIZATION,** which would lead to him receiving his final Naturalization Document like that of my Grandpa Samuel Hiller. Then again, they may have been lost to time.

I was, however, still confused. How did my Grandfather Morris Ruderman, from the tiny shtetl of Kraisk (in Lithuania prior to World War I), make his way to the United States? I hoped that someone would read and answer the question I posed on the **GENEALOGY.COM** website under the **category of LITHUANIA**. In August 2007, I received a very detailed explanation of what that journey may possibly have entailed from kind man, John Peters. His email, correcting my interpretation of the information regarding the ship on which Grandpa Morris may have sailed, should be of interest to many readers whose ancestors came from this area, but could not find their actual passage to America.

August 25, 2007

Labas (Lithuanian for 'hi') Liz,

There was no S.S. Bulgaria arrival in April of 1900. The S. S. Belgravia may have arrived, (i.e. dropped anchor) on April 17 and perhaps even had the passengers inspected on that date, but it was typical for passengers not to be admitted to the U.S. until a later date. Between 1892 and 1924, steerage passengers were ferried to Ellis Island where they were 'processed', i.e., inspected, questioned, examined physically and mentally, etc. First and second class passengers had all that done on board the ship, and once they 'passed' the inspection and examination, they were immediately ferried either to the train depot in New Jersey where many immigrants went after leaving Ellis Island or to New York City. If there were many ships arriving on a given day, the inspectors might not get to inspect the ship for a day or more. So, it may be that your grandfather remembered more the date he was admitted to the U.S., which might well have been April 20.

On the other hand, I have found the dates reported by ancestors to be notoriously unreliable, sometimes off by several years…I have gone over every passenger name on the manifest of the ship my grandfather came on, several times, very carefully, and cannot find his entry. I can only conclude that he incorrectly remembered the ship name or the date or the year.

Many records also do not note the town or village name from which the person emigrated, but rather the 'state' or 'province' in which it is located. This is especially true for Kaunas and Vilnius, which were both cities and provinces much as New York is both a city and a state.

The majority of emigrants from Lithuania in the late 1800s and early 1900s traveled by train to their port of embarkation. The most common route was the railroad west from Kaunas through Virbalis into East Prussia (a province of Germany), then south at Insterberg or Koenigsburg to Hamburg, Bremen, Rotterdam, etc. along the Atlantic Coast. A few went to the port of Libau on the Baltic coast.

These emigrants would go to one of the many train stations in Lithuania by bus, by horse or ox-drawn cart or even by boatlift if they lived on a canal or river. Russians had a well developed and readily accessible rail system at the turn of the 20th century.

So, your grandfather did not go by boat from Kaunas to New York, but he did leave Europe by boat.

Welcome to the challenging world of genealogy.

John Peters

This was all so fascinating and so well written and detailed, I could close my eyes and imagine my own ancestors making the journey of a lifetime across Eastern Europe on their way to America.

New York Is A Wonderful Town...

It was exhilarating when, checking the **1920 Census** on **ANCESTRY.COM** for Wasserman, I found Jack and Dorothy Wasserman living in Brooklyn, New York. Further research in the **1930 Census** showed the Wassermans still in Brooklyn where they now had two daughters, Sylvia and Blossom. Discovering this rather uncommon name, Blossom became my touchstone with my Dad's maternal family, the Cohens.

The 1930 **Census** contains information which I found helpful in my search for Dorothy Wasserman's mother, whom I suspected was the older sister of my Grandma Sarah Cohen Ruderman. The Census listed Dorothy and Jack's ages at their marriage as 17 and 22, respectively. Doing some simple math, I established that Dorothy was born in 1902 or 1903 and placed their marriage in 1918 or 1919. I also learned the birth years of their children – Sylvia in 1920 and Blossom in 1925. Now I could search **The New York City Marriage Records** with some accuracy. I was aware that there should be parents names listed on the certificates of marriage and hoped it would lead me to the discovery of another ancestor.

All of my known immigrant Ruderman ancestors came through Ellis Island, and, to my knowledge, they had lived in New York City, Manhattan to be specific, upon entering the United States. New York state and city have a wealth of locations where archives are stored including the **NEW YORK PUBLIC LIBRARY**(NYPL); **NYC.gov** for birth, death and marriage Indexes; **NEW YORK BIOGRAPHICAL and GENEALOGICAL SOCIETY** (NYB&S); **NEW YORK STATE VITAL RECORDS**; **NEW YORK CITY VITAL RECORDS**; and the **NEW YORK CITY BRIDES** and **NEW YORK CITY GROOMS** lists to name a few if you are searching in the five boroughs of New York. When you are uncertain exactly which website to use, **GOOGLE** is often the perfect tool. I typed New York City marriages and found the BRIDES AND GROOMS WEBSITES. Surprisingly, when I logged in to either site, I found myself viewing the **ITALIAN GENEALOGY** website. In conjunction with the **GERMAN GENEALOGICAL** SITE, the two have been responsible for having placed thousands Of records for marriages in all five boroughs of New York City between 1864–1937. After 1937 marriages were no longer required to be registered with the New York City Health Department. All marriages in New York City that are post 1938 are recorded with the clerk in the borough in which the marriage took place.

It is easy to use this website; there are five boroughs from which to choose and either exact surname spellings or sounds-like. I was unsuccessful using the Brides' site, however, when I tried the Grooms' section, I came up with several choices, one of which was the marriage of Jacob Wasserman, Kings County(Brooklyn) on October 21, 1919 and the certificate number. For a fifteen dollar credit card charge, one of the first for which I would choose to pay, I filed a **Request for a Search and Certified Copy Online.** Within a month, I received the coveted marriage certificate. AH-HA, again. This was a true find. Dorothy's parents were listed as Herman Kahn and Ceclia Cohen. Equally exciting was that Dorothy was born in the same little hamlet as my Dad – Haven, New York in Sullivan County, New York. Perhaps I would be able to locate her birth records one day. I would begin looking for her somewhere in the **Census Records**.

JEWISHGEN@LYRIS.ORG put me in touch with people around the world whose skills at researching far surpassed my own. There are translators and experts on people, places and things. My queries have been answered from people from Israel, Australia, Argentina, Ireland

and Italy just to name a few countries. I wrote about the Wasserman and Cohen/Kahn families and received an unexpected reply.

A young man in his thirties responded to my inquiry. He mentioned that his aunt, Sylvia Wasserman Schwarz had attended his Bar Mitzvah many years earlier. He also remembered her sister, with the unforgettable name, Blossom! He revealed that Sylvia had lived in the New York City area. **ANCESTRY.COM's U.S PUBLIC RECORDS INDEX** displayed a listing complete with address and telephone number and miraculously, it included a birth year for Sylvia. I had a MATCH and checked with my trusty **WHITEPAGES.COM** for confirmation of the telephone number.

Sylvia, another of my first cousins now in her eighties, was more than pleasantly surprised to learn of our family connection. It had been decades since she had been in touch with anyone connected with the Cohen family. Unfortunately, her sister, Blossom, Blossom's husband and son had passed away years earlier. She knew very little about her grandparents and regrettably had no pictures of either of them. Neither she, nor her sister, had saved or had seen any personal family records. Sylvia knew that her grandmother, Ceclia died either during or shortly after Dorothy's birth. This was the extent of the knowledge she had of her grandmother. On a much brighter note, Sylvia and her late husband, had two children; there also were several grandchildren near my son, Michael's age. We have been corresponding and I hope to meet my extended family on a future trip back East. Together, Sylvia and I did confirm that the youngest of the Cohen immigrants, our Aunt Eleanor, whom I knew as a child, came to America sometime after her sister Ceclia's death to help care for her niece, Dorothy. These records remain unfound, but certainly not for trying. Aunt Eleanor Cohen remained unmarried and died in a tragic accident while crossing the street near her home.

Random Acts Of Kindness

When I began searching for my grandparents, Morris and Sarah Ruderman and their children, I decided to explore the last released **UNITED STATES CENSUS RECORDS,** for 1930. It was exciting to find my first family record in July of 2006. At this point I discovered the truths, as well as the inconsistencies, which were contained even in official documents.

By 1930, Grandpa Morris owned a home and a butcher shop on Jersey Avenue in Port Jervis. Indeed, his occupation was described as Retail Merchant/Butcher. Both my Dad and his sister, Rae, worked in the family business. Aunt Rae was the bookkeeper; on the other hand, I found it humorous that my Dad's job description was listed as a 'chauffeur,' as he drove an old truck and delivered meat around the area for Grandpa Morris. Remembering my Dad's sense of humor, I'm certain that the title was his idea! Finally, I observed that my other aunt, Ceil Baron, continued to live with her family along with her young daughter, Edith. She was quite young at the time of her marriage (which apparently did not last long) and with a young child, remained with her family.

A huge discrepancy was the immigration dates for both of my grandparents. I was advised that they arrived separately, in 1898 and 1900, so why did the Census show both arriving in 1905? I needed to go back in time to find the truth.

It was equally easy to find the 1920 UNITED STATES CENSUS. I did find that the family was living further up the street at 112 Jersey Avenue, but more importantly, Morris was shown as coming to America in <u>1900</u>, and that he became naturalized in 1916. This was additional information about which I was previously unaware. Knowing that both of my grandparents were here for the **1910 UNITED STATES CENSUS,** made it my next stop on the journey back in time.

I was frustrated at not being able to locate any listing for Morris or Sarah Ruderman or any of their children in the 1910 Census through **ANCESTRY.COM.** At this early stage of my researching, I reached out to the 'experts' through **JEWISHGEN.ORG**'s **S**pecial **I**nterest **G**roup. Within days, I received a reply via email from another researcher, like myself, who wanted to pass along helpful tips. Carol suggested that I join the **NEW YORK GENEALOGICAL AND BIOGRAPHICAL SOCIETY,** where I would have access to **PROQUEST,** another research tool. I could find information not available on the **ANCESTRY.COM** indexes. She had already researched the 1910 Census for me (these are the Random Acts of Kindness performed by researchers all over the world for one another. It was my hope that I, too would become proficient enough one day to be able to give back to someone who was having difficulty finding his family.)

Several surprises awaited me, when I viewed the results of that 1910 Census. Our family surname was misspelled RUDDERMAN, with two Ds, and the family was living in the Township of MAMAKATING, (of Indian derivation) which included the hamlet of Haven. This was truly the country life, being situated in an area of New York state filled with rich Revolutionary and Civil War History.

The town of Mamakating was organized in 1877. Forts were constructed all along the old mine road to protect settlers from hostile Indians. Three forts were built in Mamakating, alone. People travelling in this area found the land fertile for planting crops, with an abundance of game for hunting, streams full of fish and virgin trees for building their homes. With the construction of the famous D&H Canal (Delaware and Hudson) the area grew prosperous. During the early 1800's, there were several hundred tanneries in Sullivan County with several in Mamakating. The leather from these tanneries was of superior quality, and during the Civil War, it was used to make boots, saddles and other leather goods for the Union Army.1

The additional information contained in the **1910 Census** answered some questions and created many new ones. With only a few years separating their arrivals in America and the taking of the census, Grandma Sarah and Grandpa Morris reported their immigration dates as 1898 and 1900,respectively. This was easier to believe than the information supplied decades later. Another name also appeared on the 1910 Census – Jacob Cohen, Grandma Sarah's brother who was fourteen years old in 1910. Although Jacob or Jack as he was to be known, was noted as 'nephew,' that detail was corrected by cousin, Edie, who knew him better than the rest of the family.

If my grandparents arrived separately, how did they meet? Did they know each other in the 'old country?' When and where were they married? Another researcher suggested that I try the **FAMILY SEARCH INTERNATIONAL GENEALOGICAL INDEX,** provided by the **FAMILY HISTORY LIBRARY** of the MORMON CHURCH. On the very first try, I came up with an **Individual Record** for Morris Ruderman, from Russia, whose parents were Isack Ruderman and Rachel Arelcad and who married Sarah Cohen on August 13, 1903 in Manhattan, New York, New York. I found the corresponding record for Sarah Cohen, whose parents were Aram and Rosa Cohen.

How Will I Know Where I'm Going, If I Don't Know Where I've Been?

The confirmation of Great Grandmother Rachel's maiden name would remain an unsolved mystery until I found all of the Ruderman siblings and their marriage certificates.

My Dad

Henry Ruderman was born in the village of Haven, New York on December 16, 1908. He was a quiet man (Mom often called him the Sphinx), who had a talent for really listening to his customers (he was the owner/operator of Henry Ruderman Pontiac, Inc. for over fifty years) and his friends. Although having a limited formal education, his great gift was knowing how to speak with people from all walks of life. "Butter could melt in his mouth," Mom loved to recall, as Dad would SCHMOOZE (Urban Dictionary: Yiddish – to make ingratiating small talk) with the old-line founding families of the town; he could also 'curse like a sailor' with the many blue collar workers, who like himself, had very little education.

Henry was the youngest of three and the only son. He was the champion of his mother who suffered a mentally abusive life with his dad, whom I believe must have had a 'Napoleon complex'. Although also short in stature, Daddy was a man with a giant heart. I had no knowledge, until after his death, of some of the unselfish acts of kindness he performed with a quiet dignity for others in need in our town.

He did have high expectations for my sister, Rona and me; living in a small town, which I referred to as Port Peyton (remember the movie and the 1960's television drama, Peyton Place?) was not always easy being one of the few Jewish families in a town of 9,000 and the child of a Jewish businessman. There was a time that I heard someone whisper, "She's a dirty Jew." Mom and Dad sometimes said that it was spoken out of jealousy.

Several years ago, while looking for family photos, I came across a tattered and disintegrating scrapbook from the 1940s. Not immediately recognizing the handwriting, I perused a letter carefully attached to the first page with the old-fashioned black corner brackets we used before 'scrapbooking' became fashionable. Dated March of 1944, the letter was the first of dozens written to my Mom and sister during World War II.

Just months from the cut-off draft age of thirty-five, Henry Ruderman was drafted into the United States Army to serve Uncle Sam. In the years since their 1938 marriage, my Dad had established his used car business in Port Jervis and was providing for his family of three.

Tucked safely away in their safe were all of my Dad's **Military Documents,** which are sources of invaluable proof for any genealogist. Luckily my Mom, the consummate saver, placed these papers and postcards in an environment where, when I found them, they showed only minor yellowing and were easily readable.

The earliest postcard, dated December 21, 1942, just weeks after Dad's thirty-fourth birthday, informed him that he had been classified 3-A-3 until further notice. He was called to duty and entered into active service on March 17, 1944 and was 'separated' or discharged from service on November 17, 1945, having served one year, eight months and one day for his nation. The day of his discharge, he received $130.90, having reached Technician Fifth Grade, and received a Good Conduct Medal, the American Theatre Service Medal and the World War II Victory Medal. Although my dad never served overseas, I was very proud of his service to his country.

These details appear on **The Army of the United States Separation Qualification Record** from which I learned, for the first time, that my Dad, although not a high school graduate, attended Ramsdall Business School in Middletown, New York for one year in 1928, helping him to attain the success he would eventually achieve as a businessman.

Dad's job was listed as a salesman of motor vehicles and supplies, trucks, tires, tubes, inspecting automobiles for defects, removing and replacing all worn parts and completely overhauling motors and repairing auto bodies.

Elizabeth Ruderman Miller

This distinction enabled him to take and complete an eight week Automotive Mechanic program in the Corps of Engineers at Fort Belvoir, Virginia, at which time he was assigned to the post of Automotive Parts Clerk where he received, stored and issued automotive parts. He checked and requisitioned parts, kept records of stock on hand, and was responsible for keeping the stock room clean and orderly.

Most meaningful of all, was a letter to my Dad from a man in the nearby town of Rio (pronounced like Ohio), New York written to my Dad shortly after his Army induction. Tom Pendell's son had shared a letter from my father about being drafted at such an advanced age. It had brought both father and son to tears. With Tom's encouraging response to my Dad, along with the heart-felt 'love letters' to my Mom, they shed a different light on the post-war Dad whom I knew and loved. I will treasure these words from a stranger as a gift of enlightenment, painting a picture of the strong, yet very sensitive man man who would become my Dad.

Excerpt from the letter dated April 25, 1944: "Henry Ruderman, dear sir – my son has allowed me to read your letter which brought both of us to tears…I look upon your calling and your soldiering as one of the calamities of war – but it is a war to sustain and perpetuate the greatest government and nation ever establishd on earth… You, Henry, have the personality of a leader and you have brains

– plenty of brains. I believe you are capable of doing better work for your nation than any 'kid' could possibly do... You care if you understand the job and will pass on to the boys in your unit an unshakeable patriotism and love for this nation better than any man I ever met in Port Jervis. I can not believe that a man of your age, with a wife and child, a home and business may push you to the front. Never the less, I would like to believe that the destiny of this nation lies in the hands of men like you – men with ability and intelligence, who stand ready to do their best... you must pursue a course that will allow you to come home with a clear conscience. You are the sort of guy that our boys will delight to serve with. You can be a mighty influence among them. Henry Ruderman, I salute you... chin up and forward to victory. Yours sincerely, Tom Pendall

I would like to believe that readers will recognize the quality of many men during this period who shared the same 'call to duty' that was representative of that 'greatest generation.'

But We're Cousins…

Growing up in a small town, especially one with a small Jewish population, made me very aware of the few members in my immediate family. I didn't give a thought to the genealogical significance of who was a first, second or third cousin until I was in my teens. Prior to those years, I just knew that they all came to my birthday parties, which were held in our backyard under the sunny skies of a warm July sun.

I had three first cousins who lived in Port Jervis along with my sister, Rona and me. My Dad's only niece, Edie, although considerably older than I, and my Mom's half-brother Ben's two sons, Harvey and Donald were slightly older than I. The remaining first cousins lived in New Jersey and were born to Mom's other brother, Nathan and his first wife. Deanna and Herbie paid us infrequent visits until their move to Hattiesburg, Mississippi. With distance and misunderstandings, our relationships dwindled. Nearly fifty years had passed when I finally found and re-established a welcomed connection with Harvey and Herb.

ANCESTRY.COM listed a Harvey Hiller in the San Diego, California area with an address and telephone number. The evening of July 5, 2007 was warm and delightful, so With portable phone and paper in hand, I settled in my comfortable patio chair and hoped that I would reach my cousin. An unfamiliar male voice answered the phone with a surprised, yet excited tone, and we spent the next two hours catching up on each others lives.

My Grandfather, Sam Hiller had adopted Ben and Sadie, Grandma Annie's children born in Poland, after their arrival in the United States in 1920. I had verified these records through **ANCESTRY.COM** and was anxious to shall of the information with my family. Although Sadie, who was much older, married and had already moved to New York City, Ben worked with Grandpa Sam in his silk mill along the Delaware River in Port Jervis. Ben, his wife Anne and their boys lived just around the corner from my Dad's Pontiac dealership, but I honestly don't remember being in their home more than a few times. Our family rift occurred some time around the death of our mutual grandparents over money - of course. However, as I was to learn from lengthy conversation with Harv, everyone remembers the facts through different eyes.

Harv and I compared our parents' stories about the Hiller and Bornstein immigration to the United States and their lives together as a blended family after 1920. I was able to contribute detailed facts from my search about which he had no knowledge. Remembering that my Mom was the 'love child' of her parents and the half-siblings may have shown some resentment about their place in the family, I listened to Harv's spin on the family relationships. This was to be one of several contradictory accounts of my family history.

Ben, Harv's dad, was Grandma Annie's biological son. I found it difficult to believe that when Ben needed proof of his immigration in order to obtain a passport to attend Harv's military wedding in England, Grandma Annie refused to help him find the papers. Ben went to our Tante Rosie (Annie's sister), who assisted him in finding the proper documents.

Harv recounted that his Dad had decided to go into sales when Grandpa Sam suffered bankruptcy and moved from Port Jervis back to Paterson, New Jersey. Ben said he would repay a $500 loan made to him to get started in business. He believed that Grandpa Sam had given him the start-up money, but Grandpas Sam barely had the money to restart his own business. My Dad, in his quiet, benevolent way, gave Grandpa the money to give to his son. Mom said that Ben never did pay back the loan, but I chose not to share this information after so many years. By this time, the past is just the past for us – no sense in stirring the pot over fifty years of misconceptions. There was 'bad blood' in our family by the 1960s, and we cousins would never see each other again. I was very sad to hear that Donald, Harv's brother, had died in his early 60's of pancreatic cancer just months before our phone conversation. Too little, too late to reach both cousins.

I received a lovely email the next day thanking me for our long chat. Harv included valuable information about his parents' and our Aunt Sadie's deaths and burials and forwarded some pictures of his family. We emailed several times during the next months. My husband, Roger, and I were planning to fly down to San Diego when I received a most upsetting email from Harv's wife, Dee, informing me that my cousin had died on February 13, 2008 of a massive coronary. At least I had made the contact before it was too late.

WHITEPAGES.COM directed me to only one name in New Jersey, which is where my Mom believed that my cousin, Herb resided. Herb was delighted to reconnect and provided the necessary information regarding his older sister, who I learned had been living in Florida for some years. We shared email addresses and continued to send facts through cyberspace. Yes, **EMAIL** has become an important tool for those of us who are researching and putting together our family histories and Trees. We no longer have to wait for the unpredictable mail to arrive with our precious pictures and details (although certain documents such as marriage certificates must arrive through the postal service).

How Will I Know Where I'm Going, If I Don't Know Where I've Been?

A few years my senior, Herb related that he was basically retired from his career as a recruiter - a profession he and my husband, Roger share in common. Herb provided a telephone number for his sister, which unfortunately was incorrect. I was most interested in learning about Deanna's three children and their families.

Ironically, a long distance friend of mine had just convinced me to sign up on **FACEBOOK.COM.** I prefer to communicate with friends in a more personal, secure manner, but agreed to try the **Facebook** website. Little did I know how timely and coincidental this decision would be. A few days after posting my bio, I heard from a young man named David, who informed me that he was Deanna's son. He supplied numerous pictures, dates and pertinent information for our Hiller ancestry. His Uncle Herb had mentioned my name, and Dave took a chance that I would be registered on **FACEBOOK.COM**. I agree – TAKE A CHANCE on avenues such as **FACEBOOK** and even **MySpace**. These websites are proven links enabling us to connect with family during these days of the Internet. When I approached the genealogical process of researching my Family Tree, I had no idea what degree of success I would or wouldn't achieve.

THE WEDDING PHOTO

ANNIE BORNSTEIN (right) and HER MOTHER,
DINA BORNSTEIN, GRITSE, POLAND,
EARLY 1900S

Henry Ruderman

Morris Ruderman

No. 295

ORIGINAL 191

UNITED STATES OF AMERICA

Department of Commerce and Labor
BUREAU OF IMMIGRATION AND NATURALIZATION
DIVISION OF NATURALIZATION

DECLARATION OF INTENTION

(Invalid for all purposes seven years after the date hereof)

State of New York }
Sullivan County } ss.

In the Supreme Court of New York

3. Morris Ruderman, aged 36 years, occupation Butcher, do declare on oath (affirm) that my personal description is: Color White, complexion dark, height 5 feet 5 inches, weight 142 pounds, color of hair brown, color of eyes grey, other visible distinctive marks none
_____; I was born in Pryzk, Vilna, Russia
on the 15th day of April, anno Domini 1879; I now reside at Kaser, New York
I emigrated to the United States of America from Kovna, Russia
on the vessel Belgoria; my last foreign residence was Pryzk, Vilna, Russia
It is my bona fide intention to renounce forever all allegiance and fidelity to any foreign prince, potentate, state, or sovereignty, and particularly to Nicholas II Emperor of all the Russias, of which I am now a subject; I arrived at the port of New York, in the State/Territory/District of New York on or about the 20 day of April, anno Domini 1901; I am not an anarchist; I am not a polygamist nor a believer in the practice of polygamy; and it is my intention in good faith to become a citizen of the United States of America and to permanently reside therein:
SO HELP ME GOD.

Morris Ruderman
(Original signature of declarant)

Subscribed and sworn to before me this ____
[SEAL.] day of February, anno Domini 1916

Geo. J. Potter
Clerk of the Supreme Court.
By _____, Clerk.

DECLARATION OF INTENTION FOR
NATURALIZATION FOR MORRIS RUDERMAN
1916

SAMUEL HILLER

Владѣлецъ книжки:

1. Имя, отчество, фамилія:

Яковъ-Шія Нусимовъ-Іосковъ

Хиллеръ

2. Званіе:

еврей

3. Время рожденія:

$\frac{15}{27}$ *Іюня 1882 г.*

или возрастъ:

PASSPORT PAGE OF SAMUEL HILLER – 1908
WRITTEN IN RUSSIAN SHOWING DATE OF
BIRTH

PORT JERVIS, NEW YORK

BORNSTEIN BROTHERS' PASSPORT PHOTO

IGI Individual Record	FamilySearch™ International Genealogical Index v5.0
	North America

Search Results | Download | Pedigree

Morris Ruderman
Male   Family

Event(s):
Birth: , Russia, Ussr
Christening:
Death:
Burial:

Parents:
Father: Isack Ruderman,   Family
Mother: Rachel Areicad Jackey

Marriages:
Spouse: Sarah Cohen   Family
Marriage: 13 AUG 1903 Manhattan, New York, New York

Messages:
Extracted marriage record for locality listed in the record. The source records are usually arranged chronologically by the marriage date.

Source Information:
Batch No.:	Dates:	Source Call No.:	Type:	Printout Call No.:	Type:
M002824					Film
Sheet:					

THE CHURCH OF JESUS CHRIST OF LATTER-DAY SAINTS
© 1999-2005 by Intellectual Reserve, Inc. All rights reserved.
English approval: 3/1999
Use of this site constitutes your acceptance of these Conditions of Use (last updated:
3/22/1996). Privacy Policy (last updated: 3/27/2006). 26
http://www.familysearch.org v.2.5.0

About Us | Contact Us | Press Room
LDS Church Sites | LDS Country Sites

FAMILY HISTORY LIBRARY – FHL MARRIAGE RECORD FOR MORRIS RUDERMAN & SARAH COHEN

No. 582835

THE UNITED STATES OF AMERICA
CERTIFICATE OF NATURALIZATION

Petition, Volume 15 Number 3694

Description of holder: Age 34 years, height 5 feet 8½ inches, color White complexion, Dark color of eyes, Brown color of hair, Black, visible distinguishing marks, None.

Name, age and place of residence of wife Annie Hiller, nee Bernstein age 26 yrs, resides at Paterson, N.J.

Names, ages, and places of residence of minor children Rose 1 yr resides at Paterson, N.J.

State of New Jersey
Passaic County

Be it remembered that Samuel Hiller, then residing at number 516 Main City of Paterson, State of New Jersey, who previous to his naturalization was a subject of Russia, having applied to be admitted a citizen of the United States of America pursuant to law, and also a regular term of the Common Pleas County of Passaic County holden at Paterson on the 16th day of June in the year of our Lord nineteen hundred and fifteen, the court having found that the petitioner had resided continuously within the United States for at least five years and in the State of New Jersey for at least one year immediately preceding the date of the filing of his petition, and that said petitioner intends to reside permanently in the United States, had in all respects complied with the law in relation thereto, and that he was entitled to be so admitted, it was thereupon ordered by the said court that he be admitted as a citizen of the United States of America.

In testimony whereof the seal of said court is hereunto affixed on the 16th day of June in the year of our Lord nineteen hundred and fifteen and of our Independence the one hundred and thirty-ninth.

CERTIFICATE OF NATURALIZATION FOR
SAMUEL AND ANNIE HILLER

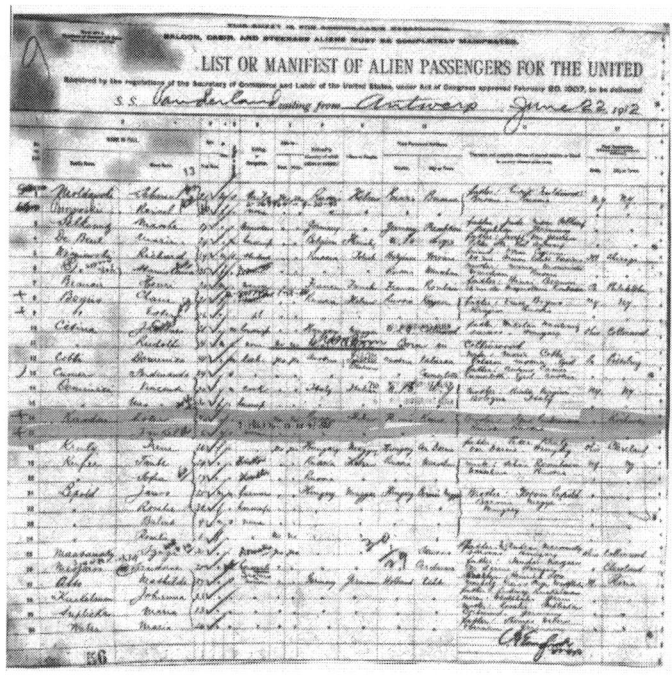

1912 SHIP'S MANIFEST – ESTHER AND JACOB KASDIN 1912

SKETCH OF HENRY RUDERMAN – UNITED STATES ARMY, 1945

Army of the United States

SEPARATION QUALIFICATION RECORD
SAVE THIS FORM. IT WILL NOT BE REPLACED IF LOST

This record of job assignments and special training received in the Army is furnished to the soldier when he leaves the service. In its preparation, information is taken from available Army records and supplemented by personal interview. The information about civilian education and work experience is based on the individual's own statements. The veteran may present this document to former employers, prospective employers, representatives of schools or colleges, or use it in any other way that may prove beneficial to him.

1. LAST NAME—FIRST NAME—MIDDLE INITIAL			MILITARY OCCUPATIONAL ASSIGNMENTS		
RUDERMAN, HENRY			10. MONTHS	11. GRADE	12. MILITARY OCCUPATIONAL SPECIALTY
2. ARMY SERIAL No.	3. GRADE	4. SOCIAL SECURITY No.	5	Pvt	Ordnance Basic Training 521
42 099 861	TEC 5	None	15	Tec 5	Parts Clerk Automotive 348
5. PERMANENT MAILING ADDRESS (Street, City, County, State)					
101 East Main St Port Jervis, New York					
6. DATE OF ENTRY INTO ACTIVE SERVICE	7. DATE OF SEPARATION	8. DATE OF BIRTH			
17 Mar 44	17 Nov 45	12 Dec 08			
9. PLACE OF SEPARATION					
Separation Point, ASFTC Fort Belvoir, Va.					

SUMMARY OF MILITARY OCCUPATIONS

13. TITLE—DESCRIPTION—RELATED CIVILIAN OCCUPATION

PARTS CLERK, AUTOMOTIVE 348

Received, stored and issued automobile parts. Checked and requisitioned parts. Took inventories. Kept record of stock on hand. Was responsible for keeping stock room clean and orderly.

HONORABLE DISCHARGE –
HENRY RUDERMAN -1945 A

HONORABLE DISCHARGE –
HENRY RUDERMAN -1945 B

ARIE & SARAH BORNSTEIN HOFNUNG.
TUVIA HOFNUNG (center) only survivor of the
holocaust TZIRA HOFNUNG

The Central Database of Shoah Victims' Names
Home | About | Holocaust-Shoah | Education | Exhibitions | Suppor
Русский | עברית

Full Record Details for **Hofnung Tzira**

Source	Pages of Testimony
Last Name	HOFNUNG
First Name*	TZIRA
Gender	Female
Date of Birth	1916
Place of Birth	WARSZA,WARSZAWA,WARSZAWA,POLAND
Permanent residence	WARSZA,WARSZAWA,WARSZAWA,POLAND
Type of material	Page of Testimony
Submitter's Last Name	HOFNUNG
Submitter's First Name	TUVIA
Relationship to victim	BROTHER
Registration date	26/04/1999

PAGES OF TESTIMONY: TRANSLATION FROM HEBREW – TZRA HOFNUNG BY HER BROTHER, TUVIA at YAD VASHEM, ISRAEL

New York Passenger Lists, 1820-1957

Name:	**Efraim Ruderman**
Arrival Date:	4 Jan 1905
Estimated birth year:	abt 1883
Age:	22
Gender:	Male
Port of Departure:	Rotterdam
Ethnicity/Race/Nationality:	Hebrew
Ship Name:	Statendam
Search Ship Database:	
Port of Arrival:	New York, New York
Line:	7
Microfilm Serial:	T715
Microfilm Roll:	T715_526
Page Number:	108

IMMIGRATION OF ABE RUDERMAN

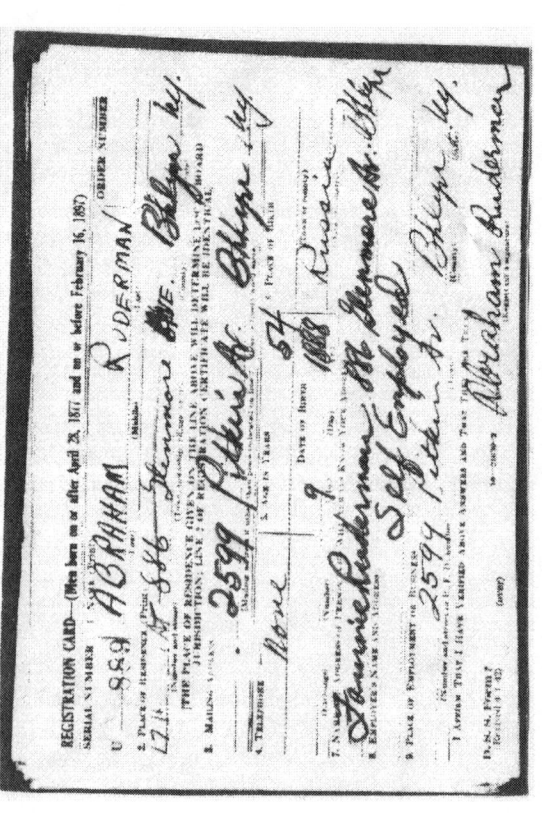

WORLD WAR II REGISTRATION CARD ABRAHAM RUDERMAN

JANUARY 4, 1905 IMMIGRATION OF EFRAIM (ABE)
RUDERMAN OF KRAISK

BORNSTEIN COUSIN FROM GRITSE, POLAND
EARLY 1900S

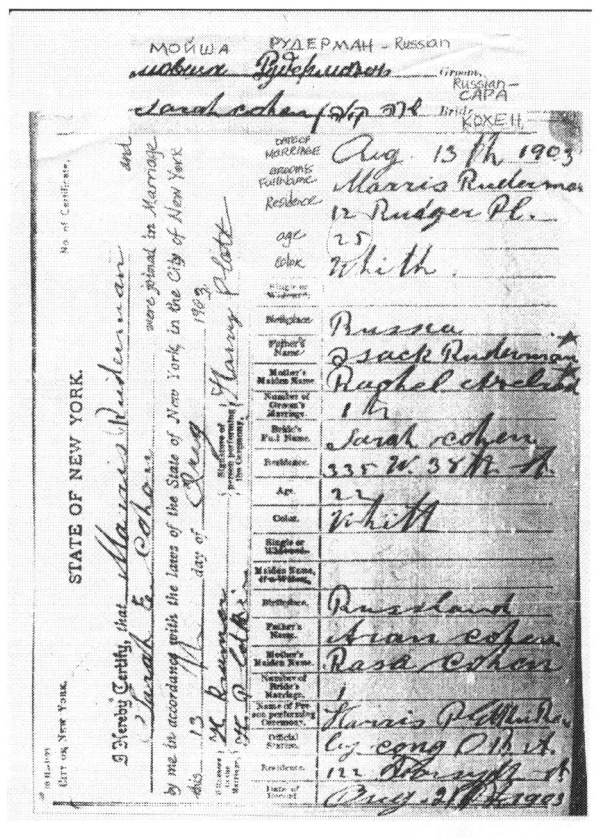

AUGUST 13, 1903 MARRIAGE CERTIFICATE OF
MORRIS RUDERMAN AND SARAH COHEN

NOVEMBER 6, 1908 MARRIAGE CERTIFICATE OF ABE RUDERMAN AND FANNIE FORMAN

1919 MARRIAGE CERTIFICATE OF JACOB WASSERMAN AND DOROTHY KAHN

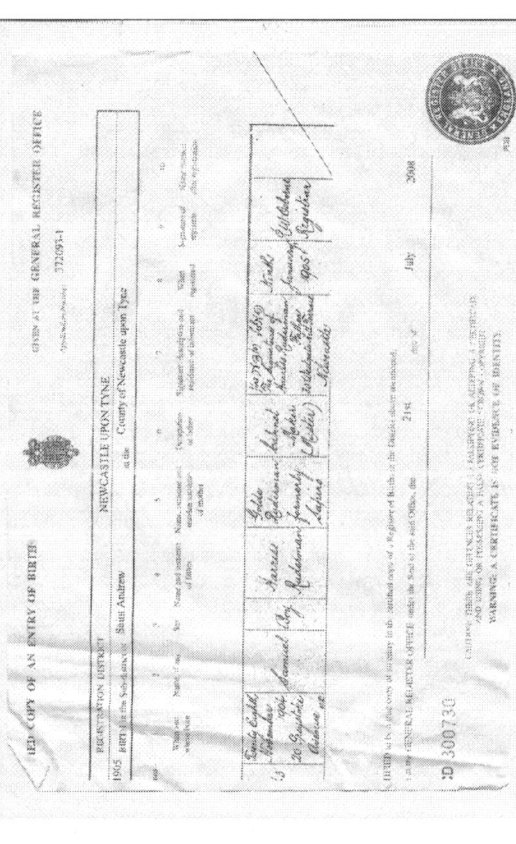

ENGLISH BIRTH CERTIFICATE – SAM RUDERMAN

First Name: *Eisig*
Last Name: *Schapiro*
Ethnicity: *Russian, Hebrew*
Last Place of Residence: *London*
Date of Arrival: *Mar 20, 1905*
Age at Arrival: *30y* Gender: *M* Marital Status: *M*
Ship of Travel: *Saint Louis*
Port of Departure: *Southampton*
Manifest Line Number: *0010*

First Name: *Golde*
Last Name: *Schapiro*
Ethnicity: *Russia, Hebrew*
Last Place of Residence: *London*
Date of Arrival: *Mar 20, 1905*
Age at Arrival: *26y* Gender: *F* Marital Status: *M*
Ship of Travel: *Saint Louis*
Port of Departure: *Southampton*
Manifest Line Number: *0021*

IMMIGRATION OF HARRY AND GOLDE RUDERMAN

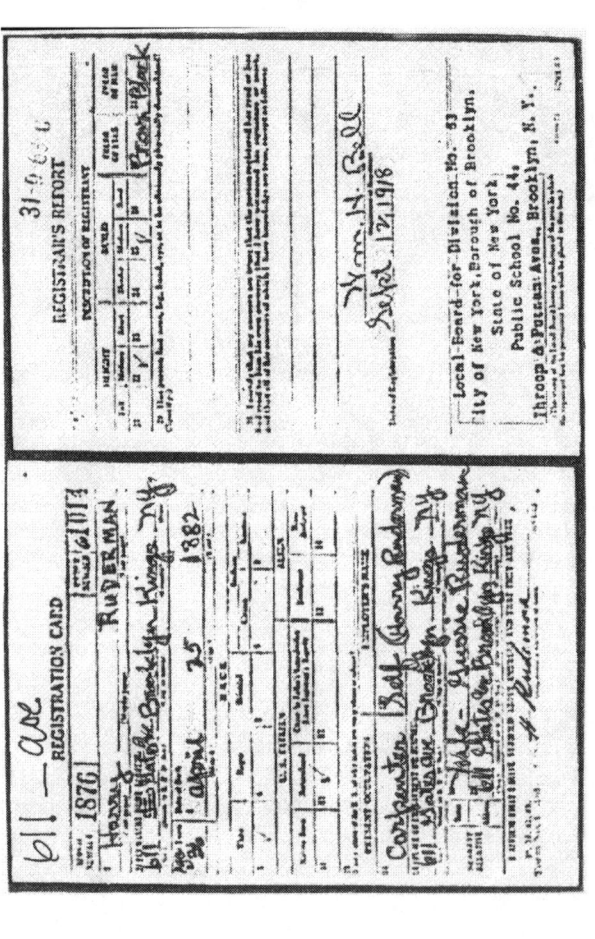

WORLD WAR I REGISTRATION CARD – HARRY RUDERMAN

Connecting History

The following wonderfully descriptive story is about my newly found cousin, Pam Hoffman's husband, Bob's uncle who grew up in 20th Century Russia and came to America to find the American dream. The story takes place in the same time period and location of my own ancestors, and transports us to a time and experiences which easily could have happened to any of my own ancestors.

Edel's grandfather was born in a shtetl in the Vilna Gubernia (district) during the reign of Nicholas the First, Czar of All the Russias, known as the 'Tyrant' by his subjects for his extreme cruelty. A proclamation was issued which served notice that all boys reaching the age of six were compelled to begin their military service in the Russian Army for a period of twenty-five years. Only the first born male was exempted.

The brothers were hidden and protected from the 'clutches of kidnapping agents of the tyrant czar', but one boy was snatched from his grandmother's arms and was never heard from again. The other two boys were forced to leave their village to avoid serving the czar in the Russian army. They travelled from village to larger village until they reached one where they were not known.

The eldest brother, Moisha, exempt from military service, decided to leave the village as there was no fear of his being apprehended. 'It is to be noted that although the brothers knew of each others; whereabouts, they failed to see each other for a space of forty years.' Moisha's father sent him to Hebrew school (chedar) led by the congregation of the Synagogue and worked for a tailor for his keep. Moisha was well liked by the Hebrew teacher (Mahlamid), who admired his industriousness and honor. Moisha was introduced to the tailor's daughter, and although they were very young, after a brief courtship, they married.

Eighteen children were born to the couple. Only six were alive when the author was sixteen; he was referred to as 'Mezzinik', the baby of the family. Although unable to educate the other children, Moisha's father pledged that he would 'do all in his power to at least try to educate one of his children.' He sent the boy to Hebrew school, and in addition provided private tutors under whose direction, the boy learned to read and write in Russian and Yiddish.

At this time, the prevailing Russian Army Service Law stipulated that all males reaching the age of 21 were compelled to serve five years in the Russian Army. This was a change for the better from the days of Nicholas the First.

It was, however the father's intention to have ALL of his sons avoid service in the Russian Army. He bribed the village record keeper to mark one of his sons 'dead' and to change his name to another who was NOT on the 'army lists.' It was necessary for this brother to leave town as well. He travelled to the safety of his two siblings.

Moisha's father decided Moisha should learn a trade, so Moisha became tailor. With the necessary skills learned, Moisha left for another town after his Bar Mitzvah, (age 13). A friend used his influence to find Moisha at a job. He chopped wood, carried buckets of water from the well, drove the cow to graze in the field, and warmed irons for pressing. All of these duties were considered 'necessary' 'skills' to become an expert tailor. Finally, he was allowed to sit at the tailor's table and learn the 'tricks of the trade'.

He progressed quickly enough that, after the end of his apprenticeship, Moisha remained with the tailor for another year, now under different terms and conditions – fifty rubles ($25)for the year, board and smokes! The following year he left for Kiev, where he worked until he received the letter informing him of his induction into the army.

In 1886, now 21, he began serving for the next three years, eight months under the 'iron hand' of Alexander the Third. He returned home, with no money in his pockets, only to find his father and mother in poor health.

As was the custom in the Russian villages and towns, a soldier who had served his time in the army and had returned, was considered very highly desirable as a matrimonial 'catch'. Marriage brokers (Sehatkrins) urged him to accompany them to view the 'fair damsels.' One of them struck his fancy; he courted her and they married in 1888. Moisha received a wedding dowry of one hundred fifty Rubles. Their first son was born in 1890.

He believed that he could not make a living for his family at home, so he contacted an uncle in America. His uncle sent a 'ship-carte'(transportation) for him, however, his wife and child remained with his parents until he could send for them. Moisha thought he was leaving for the 'home of plenty and freedom' as they understood the United States to be from letters they read.

There was an 'immigration rush' at this time by Russian Peasants partly because of their harsh treatment and also they believe they could expect 'sudden riches' in their 'new country.' A proclamation was issued that no one was to leave Russia under the penalty of exile to Siberia. It was necessary to bribe guards patrolling the Russian Border. This was successfully accomplished by the transportation agents, The 'Russian Sentries' either turned their backs or conveniently disappeared for a time, thus giving the people a chance to run across the border.

Moisha arrived at 'Castle Garden'(the destination before the opening of Ellis Island) in 1890. Benjamin Harrison was President of the United States. A short time later, the country felt the grip of an economic crisis. factories were closed and people were unemployed. Charitable groups helped by distributing food and clothing to couples and their dependents, but ignored single people, such as himself. Moisha shoveled snow for twenty cents an hour. People suffered terrible hardships and heartaches. It was a rude awakening to this 'golden land, the home of plenty' which he had imagined.

Four years later, he was a worker receiving five dollars per week. Living conditions were terrible, but he managed to save enough to send for his wife and son, who joined him in 1896. He became 'naturalized' and received his papers on September 17, 1896. They resided on Orchard Street, in the heart of the Lower East Side. Both of his Children attended and graduated from public schools and went on to successful careers. Excerpts from **THE GENEALOGICAL RECORD OF THE HOFFMAN FAMILY 1781 – DATE.** "Dictated by my uncle, Edel Hoffman (1866) from memory and records in his possession and translated by me, Morris Hoffman (1899)." Reproduction granted by Robert Hoffman.

Genealogy Without Documentation Is Mythology

Those of us who are passionate about searching for our roots appear to have one thing in common – WANTING TO PRESERVE A LEGACY for our children and future generations. This was especially apparent when Pam Hoffman and I found each other. We continued to connect every dot until we experienced our 'Ah-ha' moment. We followed the twists and turns of first reading each others **emails,** followed by numerous cross-country **phone calls** listening to each others' accounts of our mostly limited knowledge about our family.

The process of obtaining official records and **proof of** verbal tales is easy one day and arduous on others. Pam and Bob Hoffman, my newly discovered cousins, had a much earlier interest in genealogy than I, having already spent years researching Pam's grandmother, Esther Ruderman.

Elizabeth Ruderman Miller

They had several documents in their possession which would be critical to my **verification process.** Pam had written to the Monroe County, New York **clerk's office,** furnishing them with Esther's **date of death** and **cemetery** location along with a fee and received the **genealogical copy,** which provided the information necessary to compare our mutual records for proof of family relationship. The official **Death Certificate** listed her father as Isaac Ruderman, her mother as Rose, an Americanized form of Ruchel or Rachel and very importantly, that Esther's birthplace was Kreiske, Russia- none other than Kraisk!

Esther Ruderman Kasdin Joseph, chronicled her stories of visiting her sibling who lived in Port Jervis, New York. My heart raced when Pam recounted Esther's tale of visiting her brother, Morris and his son, Henry! **AH-HA!!!** THEY were my grandfather and father. Esther also mentioned her visits with her sister, Sophie Ruderman Chefeitz who lived across the bridge from Port Jervis in Matamoras, Pennsylvania. Her marriage to Louis Chefeitz produced two daughters and a son. Daughter Rachel married Max Lafer and gave birth to a daughter, Shirley and a son, William who lived in the town of Greenville, just outside of Port. I was unaware of ALL of these names until I went to my two main 'squeezes' – my Mom and my cousin, Edie, who lived with my grandparents until she was married.

During her childhood while living with our grandparents, Edie spoke Yiddish with the family. This story triggered her memory enough, that she remembered a woman who was referred to, in Yiddish, as 'Esta Kasha,' who was indeed, our Grandfather Morris' sister, Esther but thought that the family on 'Heater's Hills' in Matamoras was a form of the name Schaeffer. This fact was proven, when I contacted the **Port Jervis Funeral Home,** for records of Sophie and Louis Chefeitz's deaths. They also used the name of Schaeffer, PERHAPS wanting to have a less Jewish-sounding surname in an area with so few Jewish families. They were both buried under the Chefeitz name.

Mom also remembered and passed on a personal story about my Dad and his cousins, which certainly explained why we had no contact in my sister's and my generation. It seems my Dad, who sold used cars before he was offered a Pontiac dealership by General Motors, had tried to 'make a deal' for his relatives. The cousin-in-law didn't feel that it was 'fair enough' and disputed the price with my father. I have heard from so many sources that my Dad was one of the most generous and fair men around, so when Dad said, "then You don't really want a car," that was that – they left without purchasing a vehicle, and they were no longer on speaking terms. Fortunately, when Pam mentioned Shirley's married name and that she had moved to Florida from Rochester, my trusty, **WHITEPAGES.COM** enabled me to find Shirley, and through her, I located her brother. I am happy to say that we had some lovely conversations. Each of them provided me with their spouses and children to add to our Family Tree. Ironically, Bill attended Port Jervis High School with my sister, Rona, unbeknownst to all but my Dad. Now, when I visit the graves of my grandparents and my Dad, I also climb the hill to place on rock on the headstones of my Aunt Rae and her husband, Max because they, too were Family.

A very helpful man from Israel explained how to use **the JEWISHGEN.ORG JEWISH NAMES DATABASE.** I checked both the countries of Belarus and Lithuania for the Americanized given name of Sophie. The information gave me several choices which, amazingly, were close enough to match the names 'Esta Kasha'. The Yiddish nickname for Sophie was Eske or Eshke or Khasha! I also discovered another Yiddish variant, SHOSHE, which would lead me to her IMMIGRATION RECORDS and **SHIP'S MANIFEST** list.

Some years earlier, a most fortuitous meeting took place in Rochester, New York. Joel Kasdin, Pam's older brother was attending a social event, when he met Shirley Lafer. Unaware of their relationship, they conversed, and the subject of having relatives in the Port Jervis area came up. Low and behold, the Kasdins and Lafers had found each other! That meeting and the information which was exchanged, enabled me, some years later, to put those pieces of our puzzle together along with mine on the Ruderman Family Tree.

How Will I Know Where I'm Going, If I Don't Know Where I've Been?

I now had some corroborating evidence of the correct family ancestors' names: Esther Ruderman Kasdin Joseph's headstone was translated by an expert at my **Temple.** The inscription confirmed that she was the daughter of **ITZCHAK,** and her **death certificate** also used the name **ISAAC** for her father and **ROSE,** certainly a form of Ruchel or Rachel for her mother. These were the corresponding names on my own grandfather, Morris' **death records,** along with the **town of KRAISK** (Kreiske or Graysk), was proof positive that we were family!

Assuming that Grandpa Morris arrived in the United States in 1900, I was anxious to find the actual **Immigration documents** for his siblings, known at the time as ABE, ESTHER, SOPHIE and HARRY. Pam had provided me with a copy of her grandmother Esther's **SHIP'S MANIFEST**, dated June, 1912. Remembering that I had a Yiddish first name indicated for Sophie, and I was positive that the family name was spelled R-U-D-E-R-M-A-N, I joined the **ELLIS ISLAND WEBSITE,** and typed in Shoshe Ruderman. 'What to my eyes would appear…', but **Schosse Ruderman, sailed on the Kroonland from Antwerp, Belgium, arriving the port of New York on February 17, 1904. She was age 24, dressmaker, Russian, and Hebrew.** Most notably, was the information that her last address was **KRAISK,** and that she was coming to her **brother MOISHE RUDERMAN, HAVEN, NEW YORK, SULLIVAN COUNTY!** This was exactly the place where my Dad was born. I double checked the record and found the identical information through **stevemorse.org.** Oddly, however, there was an additional **Record of Detained Alien Passengers** for that same passage which included Schosse Ruderman, being met by her brother, Moishe, this time with the address, **39 Jackson Street, NYC.** I hoped that this address might show up in future listings, but for now I had clear-cut proof of three members of my Ruderman family, Grandpa Morris and his two sisters, Esther and Schosse soon to become, Sophie and many of their descendants.

The Power Of Whitepages.Com

Before I acquired any proficiency with a computer, I sat down with pen and paper to list all of the family members with whom I was familiar. I recalled two visits by my Dad's cousin, Sam Ruderman and his wife, Nina when I was a young girl. The memory is so vivid, I'm certain, because Dad and Sam shared the same beautiful blue eyes, and had a striking resemblance to each other, now confirmed by other relatives. Mom also remembered that they travelled from Brooklyn to Port Jervis to buy a new car from my Dad. She also recalled they had two daughters, and I wondered why the kids never accompanied their parents on the two hour trip 'to the country' which was often how our part of the state was referred to by people in New York City - to us, 'the city.' Leafing through one of her **personal telephone books** dating back to the 1960s, Mom located Sam and Nina's address with a notation that Sam died, and Nina and her second husband, Nathan had moved to Miami,

Florida. As fortune would have it, there WAS an address and phone number added to the entry. At least forty years had passed, but I decided to take a chance see if there was a current listing for Nathan and Nina in Florida, hoping I could find a match.

WHITEPAGES.COM had a listing with the same address and Telephone number, so I placed my **first** family call in early October, 2006. When a woman answered, I asked if I was speaking with the former Nina Ruderman, widow of Sam. I'm certain she was taken aback, so I introduced myself as the daughter of Henry Ruderman, the Pontiac dealer from Port Jervis, New York. She remembered my Dad, but not meeting Mom or me. I had so many questions, but tried to speak slowly and clearly, as she informed me that her hearing, as well as her eyesight, were not good. Nina corrected me, explaining that she had a son living in Southern California and a daughter, Ronda, living in Seattle, Washington, both of whom were so very close to my own age. I couldn't believe that we had never met as children. She provided me with both telephone numbers, which I immediately copied into the notebook which I had begun. It was simply titled, <u>MY RUDERMAN FAMILY</u>. She sadly informed me that Sam had died in September, 1966 of cancer, the same disease which would take my Dad in 1983.

Nina asked if I knew of Sam's sister, Lillian. I did not. Lillian Ruderman Fenster did have two daughters, Ellen and Thelma. Ellen was writing and Thelma was teaching in higher education. I was very impressed with their credentials, and hoped I would have a meaningful conversation with each some day in the future. Although the information was not detailed, it was a place to begin. I thanked Nina profusely, gave her my telephone number and address, and asked her to call if she recollected additional Ruderman names.

I suspected there was a high incidence of cancer in the Ruderman family. With my own medical problems, I began to realize the importance of knowing family health histories and inherited genetic conditions. Both my Dad and his father died of lung cancer as the result of smoking cigars, pipes and cigarettes. Even my maternal grandfather succumbed to cancer. My mother, fortunately won the war with uterine cancer. Sharing the discoveries of medical diagnoses through genealogical research can be of vital importance to your newly found family members. EDUCATE MEMBERS ON HEALTH ISSUES. THE INFORMATION COULD AID IN THE DIAGNOSIS, TREATMENT OR UNDERSTANDING OF MEDICAL CONDITIONS.

Having additional names, I started a chart – simple at first with <u>new family names</u> listed vertically on the page. Along the top of the page, I had a space for <u>telephone numbers</u>, <u>addresses</u>, <u>date of birth</u> and <u>miscellaneous</u>. I would soon have supplemental pages as I collected more details.

My next phone call was to Robert, Nina and Sam's son who is only slightly older than I, but had retired to the beach area south of Los Angeles. It was almost immediately after my introduction, that I realized that Bob had no interest in pursuing the subject of our family connection. It would be the FIRST, but not the last disappointment in my search. **REMEMBER – NOT EVERYONE WANTS TO FIND LONG, LOST FAMILY AND EXPLORE THEIR GENERALGY**! Although a bitter pill to swallow, I would remind myself of this motto every so often.

Knocked down but not out, I proceeded to call the phone number Nina had given me for her daughter, Ronda. I left a message, hoping that I would received a call back, and indeed, I did. Ronda and I spoke so easily that it was difficult to believe that this was our first contact. She didn't recall that either of her parents had ever mentioned us 'country cousins'. Our chats would begin to connect some of the puzzle pieces. Abe Ruderman, Ronda's grandfather was my Grandpa Morris' youngest brother. In follow-up emails wishing me good luck with my project, Ronda remembered additional information about Abe's family which would be critical to my research project. It was noteworthy that Ronda **identified** Abe's wife, her Grandmother Fannie and possibly her grandfather on the 1938 Wedding photo. Step by step, I was making progress and obtaining the confirmation I

How Will I Know Where I'm Going, If I Don't Know Where I've Been?

needed. By telephone and email, I met an entirely new part of the family.

Abe and Fannie Ruderman had three children - Samuel, Lillian (Fenster) and Edith (Kresel). This branch lived in Queens while their children were young. Parts of this branch even lived together. My desire to locate their **1940 United States Census** records will be delayed until their release to the public in 2012. Ronda remembered being an attendant in one of her cousin's weddings. Like so many of us, they, too drifted apart later in life.

Years ago, many immigrant families either made the journey together, or most certainly, ended up living in large family units due to financial difficulties, language or simply because they were blood. Grandparents, aunts, uncles or cousins lived together, shared holidays and each others lives on a daily basis. Our **'Baby Boomer'** generation **moved away from the nest, leaving their core families sometimes thousands of miles to begin new job opportunities new lives and**. THIS REALIZATION AND OBSERVATION BECAME CENTRAL TO THE DIFFICULTY OF FINDING EXTENDED FAMILY MEMBERS. WE HAD LOST TRACK OF THEM, AT WORST HAD NO COMMUNICATION AT BEST.

I now had links with two of the original Ruderman siblings who had emigrated at the birth of the 20th century - Moshe/Morris and his brother, Abe who was in attendance for the 1938 Wedding photo. There would be so much more to learn about Abe and his family in the weeks and months to come.

Hoping that I would be more successful finding facts on Abe Ruderman, I noted the topics on which I would begin searching: **IMMIGRATION, CENSUS RECORDS, MARRIAGE DATES, SOCIAL SECURITY DEATH INDEX, MILITARY RECORDS** and **NAME CHANGES**.

Census statistics seemed to be a good starting point, since I had authentic names and addresses.

A My Name Is Abe

The name Abe or Abraham Ruderman is quite common, as Rudermans go. More surprisingly, though were the many listings for the surname, Ruderman, as I was under the impression that Ruderman was rare. There had to be a systematic way of finding my Grandpa Morris' youngest brother. A message appeared on the **Belarus SIG DISCUSSION GROUP(part of JEWISHGEN.ORG)** on January 13,2007 which would be the clue I needed.

A woman wrote in commenting that she had spent some time looking through the **Lithuanian Given Names Database,** discovering that the legal origin of **Avraham** was the name **EFRAIM.** With this name I was ready to search **ANCESTRY.COM** and **STEVEMORSE.ORG** for all emigrants named **Efraim Ruderman.** After weeks of getting nowhere searching for Abe Ruderman, I hit the jackpot!

EFRAIM RUDERMAN arrived in New York on January 4, 1905 having sailed on the S.S. Statendam out of Rotterdam. Already a tailor at the age of 22, he crossed the Atlantic to join his brother, at **39 Jackson Street, NYC**. There was that address again.

Having already located two of Abe, formerly Efraim's granddaughters, Ellen and Ronda, I knew that he had married a woman named Fannie, whose picture both girls had identified in Mom and Dad's **Wedding Photo.** Checking with **THE NEW YORK CITY BRIDES** and **THE NEW YORK CITY GROOMS** lists, I received a duplicate, official copy of their **CERTIFICATE AND RECORD OF MARRIAGE** from the State of New York, dated October 25, 1908 in Manhattan. I was able to inform my cousins that their grandmother's maiden name was Foorman, perhaps misspelled, and above all, I had another validation for my great-grandparents names. Abe entered his parents names as **Issac Ruderman** and **Rachel Axelroad, perhaps a form of Axelrod.** There was no doubt about it; I was filling in the branches of the Ruderman Tree.

Abe's **World War II Registration Card** from 1942, which I found on **ANCESTRY.COM,** suggests he was born in 1888; his **Marriage Certificate,** states that his birth year was 1886; and adding to the confusion is the **SHIP'S MANIFEST,** which puts his birth in 1883! Our ancestors often had no actual confirmation or paper trail of important events, especially in small shtetls, so it's anyone's guess, which of these date is fact. If Abe is the youngest sibling, my guess would be that he was born sometime between 1886 – 1888.

Emails from Ellen and Ronda after our 'meeting' online shed light on the third of Abe and Fannie Ruderman's children, Edith, who married Nathan Kresel. Ronda provided me with the names of their children, and Ellen offered some personal information on them, including last know addresses. I was hopscotching between performing searches on both sides of my family, and did not find the Kresels until mid 2008.

The U.S. Public Records Index on **ANCESTRY.COM** had a listing for sister Barbara, who was delighted to hear from me, assisting me with connections for her sister, Carol and her younger brother, Mark, who proved to be the 'baby' of the Ruderman family, chronologically, in our generation. Barbara passed along my telephone number, and bright and early the next morning, a Saturday, I heard the exuberant voice of my cousin, Mark, who was as thrilled as I to be learning of our family relationships. We chatted for two hours that first day, exchanging stories, information and finally emailing pictures. I also had a lovely introduction to his sister, Carol, sometime later. Best, of all, was an amazing visit with Mark at our home several months later. He came prepared with more recent pictures of all of his extended family members and a treasure of his grandparents – Abe and Fannie Ruderman's WEDDING PICTURE.

Mark, my teddy bear of a cousin, who is a well-known maker of celebrity bird houses, and I had an instant connection and hope to travel together one day to the birth place of our Ruderman ancestors – Kraisk, Belarus.

Don't Wait Too Long

TAKE A BREAK occasionally from collecting all of your facts and putting them to paper. That's exactly what I did one day during the week of March 12, 2009. I had a name fixed in my mind for a few days, and decided to search for the still missing portion of my Grandma Annie Bornstein Hiller's family.

After an evening telephone call with my Mom, I was aware that within the last three years of my research, my Mom's memory has been critical to my progress. She was now, at 95, beginning to show signs of forgetfulness and some confusion. Although not unusual at this advanced age, without her incredible memory and recollection of the past, I would never have been able to begin, let alone come so far in the discovery of my roots and extended family.

I REMIND YOU AGAIN – TALK TO YOUR AGING RELATIVES! It is from them you will extract the elements of your family's history. Begin with the facts, any facts, especially if you are first or second generation Americans. **INTERVIEW EVERYONE** possible – **VIDEO OR TAPE RECORD THEIR VOICES** if possible. Don't loose the precious memories of your ancestry.

Mom had given me the name of a Bornstein relative she thought might have been a professor at San Jose State in Northern California. Somehow, that tip became misplaced or at least, misfiled. **STAY ORGANIZED.** Remember to file even small pieces of paper. Whatever works for you is fine, but file IMMEDIATELY, eliminating the possibility of losing an important piece of information as I almost did.

What did I do before I discovered **WHITEPAGES.COM** online? Although not completely foolproof, it assists you in narrowing your searches on a nationwide and spelling basis. My search began in San Jose, the obvious choice for someone teaching at a university in that city. **WHITEPAGES.COM** allows you to search an entire or partial name in a specific city and state or NO state at all. This process leads to the **US SEARCH** site, where you will view ALL of the people with the 1. NAME you are searching, 2. all of the CITIES for that name, 3. possible RELATIVES for that person, 4. sometimes an AGE, 5. check mark for available PHONE and ADDRESS and 6. a **VIEW DETAILS** – enabling you to PAY FOR the premium information possibly available. During the course of searching for some relatives, this **PAY FOR** service was invaluable as you will see in several chapters.

With three city choices, I used **WHITEPAGES.COM,** selecting my cousin's first and last name for each city. **DON'T FORGET THAT YOU CAN ALSO USE JUST AN INITIAL FOR THE GIVEN NAME**. I dialed the first of two numbers with no success. A male voice answered the second number, and after exchanging some specific information, we agreed that we were related. After some disappointing telephone discoveries, I am now prepared for rejection, but in this instance, cousin Bob was eager and excited to share and learn more. We decided to speak over the weekend after Bob had time to digest all of the family history and the attachments I sent him over the next few days.

Reconnecting over the weekend led to reports about family member about whom neither of us were aware. Yes, I was about to uncover those "skeletons' in my closet. At times like these, we appreciate the reality of the expression, **two sides to every story***!*

These stories happened almost one hundred years ago, making it impossible to verify the facts as nothing was 'written in stone' back then. However, they seemed plausible with the disparity of family accounts and the reality that our families became estranged **for some reason!** I listened intently as Bob narrated HIS version of the family's life in Grojec and the first years in their newly adopted country.

After settling in Paterson, New Jersey and becoming part of the silk industry in 1909, Schyja and Abram, now

Sam Hiller and Abe Bornstein were expected to send money back to their families in Gritse when it was possible. I will never know if Sam's first wife died first or if he received an official divorce from her. During those days, an Orthodox Jew could obtain a religious divorce through the Synagogue, rather than in the civil court. This was called a *Get*. The latter resolution was the more probable solution for both Sam and Abe. Sam asked for Annie Bornstein's (Abe's sister)hand in marriage and began preparing for her journey to America. **HERE IS WHERE THE RIFT BEGAN**!

I digress a moment to explain the discovery of our family surnames which help to confirm individual connections. My cousin, Murray Hiller who resides in Atlanta, forwarded an amazing record of **Vital Records:** ***births, deaths and marriages*** from Grojec during the late 19th and early 20th centuries. This file contained several variant spellings for the surnames Hiller and Bornstein. learned that there was no letter H in the Yiddish alphabet. It's place was taken by the letter G. When I found the surnames, Giler and Giller, they translated in Hiller. The given name were a different story. Thankfully, Murray was able to translate the Yiddish names into English for me.

Discovering the correct spelling of Bornstein was more challenging. While charting the surnames I found multiple spellings any one of which could be the correct form for my family in the Warsawa Gubernia (province of Russia- Poland before World War I. Three of the most popular spellings were Borenstein, Borensztejn and Borensztajn. When I applied the given names I had for my Great Grandmother Dina and my Aunt Ruchel (Tante Rosie) I had another AH-HA moment. The revelation of your own family is thrilling. Although some names were altered when they came to America, I now had the knowledge of additional Eastern European genealogical fact to give to my family.

The Hiller and Bornstein families grew up in the small shtetl (village)of Gritse, Poland. As the story was spun by my newly found cousin Bob, Sam had refused to donate his portion for the entire Bornstein/Hiller clan, who likely lived together for financial reasons. Instead, he saved his hard earned wages for Annie's passage to America. AH – TRUE LOVE! Annie arrived in 1912 to marry Sam, leaving her own two children behind to join after she was settled. World War I intervened; it wasn't until July 12, 1920, eight long years later that the children of the combined household – Sam's son, Annie's son and daughter and Abe's three sons, were reunited with their parents. Sam and Abe had both remarried. Each were the parents of American born daughters by that date. The possible tragedy was that without Sam's monetary contribution, life was even worse for the family remaining in Poland. As Bob's story progresses, PERHAPS Abe's first wife starved to death, giving what she had to her children as any good mother would have done. I felt guilty hearing this accounting and knew that I could not relate this story to my elderly mother.

Elizabeth Ruderman Miller

It would be more that distressing to imagine this happening when she idolized her father and mother. The hardships of their youth and the bravery of their voyages to America were enough for a young child to believe about her beloved parents. This version is, of course, unsubstantiated. The young immigrants gradually stopped seeing each other. As in so many families, resentment, misunderstandings and MONEY are the roots of all evil- in this case the future generations lost their connection with their extended families.

Bob reported that he had a younger sister living on the East Coast. Within a few days, I was having a most pleasant and INFORMATIVE conversation with Mimi. She was pleased to receive my call, and we immediately delved into details of our families. As we recounted the tales, both renditions of the Bornstein sagas began in Gritse, but I was astonished at the marked contrast in our versions.

I admit that I was shocked at hearing the following, but realized that we should not judge others, especially under the circumstances in which our ancestors lived in the late 19th century Eastern Europe and early 20th century America when conditions were generally in a deplorable state. We would disapprove of what people had to do to survive in today's world. Perhaps part of this story is told for those reasons. After almost one hundred years, the truth is a part of history which is buried with our ancestors.

How Will I Know Where I'm Going, If I Don't Know Where I've Been?

Mimi's accounting of her Grandfather Abe begins as does my own version with our grandfathers' journey together to the United States. I was able to verify their passage on **ANCESTRY.COM.** This was one of my first great discoveries **proving** my grandfather's arrival in America. It was a cold, wintry voyage for both men who are listed together on the **SHIP'S MANIFEST** of the SS Main which departed Bremen, Germany on December 31, 1908 arriving at Ellis Island on January 12, 1909. The record confirmed that they both lived in Grojec, and that their final destination was Paterson, New Jersey, where they hoped to live the American Dream. It was not until this discovery that my Mom actually remembered, or was willing to discuss Grandpa Sam's decision to leave behind his wife and young son, only to divorce her a short time later to marry my grandmother. Both first wives were listed on the **SHIP'S MANIFEST** and were also written in the coveted 1908 **Passport.**

The most disturbing accounting from Mimi was regarding my Uncle Abe's treatment of his own sons. It was cruel of him to deny his immigrant sons their right to an education, however, he made the boys work in the silk factory for some time. Most unthinkable, however, was what followed. Abe, his second wife, Annie, and their daughter, Sylvia, lived in an apartment along with his sons. Early one morning, Abe, Annie and Sylvia deliberately moved out of their apartment, leaving their sons behind to fend for themselves. This is unconscionable to me. Mimi confirmed Mom's account that one of the brothers died in an accident. She added that a second committed suicide. They were two young boys who came to America with hope in their hearts. Both died so tragically before the prime of their lives. Cousins Bob and Mimi were the children of Abe's remaining son, Irving, my Mom's first cousin, whom she affectionately called Issy.

On a typically foggy, San Francisco day, which I've missed since my college years in the Bay Area, my husband, Roger and I had the joy of meeting my cousin, Bob Bornstein for the first time over Memorial Day weekend 2009. During our short, but sweet visit, we hugged, drank Turkish coffee, viewed old pictures and crammed some sixty years of getting acquainted into a few brief hours. New family friendships were certainly forged that day.

All In The Family

I was very excited at the thought of locating the the descendants of my Great Uncle Abe Bornstein's daughter, Sylvia. Sylvia had two sons, Theodore and David. The prospect of completely identifying and knowing descendants of my great grandparents, Tuvia and Dina Borensztejn was an impossible dream just three years ago. Now, the only obstacle in front of me was discovering two men whose location was a mystery.

Sylvia Bornstein and Henry Englander had two sons, Ted and David, who grew up in New Jersey and both of whom had careers with the Postal Service. I set my sights on finding these two brothers, whom I hoped would still reside in the Garden State - making things easy for a change.

As with most first born American generations in my family, I first checked the **SOCIAL SECURITY DEATH INDEX** for Sylvia Englander, my Mom's first cousin who was born in 1917. The **SSI** confirms *dates of birth* and at least the *month* and *year* of death along with the last *residence* where the person most probably collected social security. Sylvia passed away not far from her birthplace of Paterson, New Jersey, yet she and Mom had not seen each other for decades. I then reviewed the **1930 UNITED STATES CENSUS,** which is, unfortunately, the last year available to us until 2012, when we will be able to view the **1940 CENSUS.** I am certain that it will contain information which will assist me in finding other family.

The official **1930 CENSUS** records are invaluable because they contain the following: Address, Name of each family member living at the address, relationship to the head of family; own or rent the property; value of property if owned; sex; race; age at last birthday; marital status; age at first marriage; birth place of person; father and mother; date of immigration date of naturalization.

It is important to remember that **AGES** and **YEARS MAY BE DECEIVING!!** Many immigrants did not know the exact date of their birth, often making it a GUESSTIMATE. The census may indicate that a person came to the United States in 1905, however, when you are fortunate enough to find the **SHIPS MANIFEST**, he may have actually arrived in 1900. The same holds true with regards to the dates of **NATURALIZATION.** The final issuing of papers is most likely about five years following the application. **DON'T ASSUME ANYTHING!**

How Will I Know Where I'm Going, If I Don't Know Where I've Been?

I prepared to locate the Englander brothers beginning with Ted. Going to my faithful, **WHITEPAGES.COM,** I copied a name in New Jersey with NO telephone number. There I was surprised to see a **view phone** sign. Instructions guaranteed an Exclusive Listing if I subscribed to become a WHITEPAGES member, and it was FREE! Free is good when several sources come with a charge. After I easily joined the network, there was a telephone number attached to Ted's name. I was taken aback when the voice at the other end of the line answered, "post office." I asked for my cousin, but was told that he had retired several years earlier. My hunch was that he may have moved to Florida, as do many Easterners. The next listing on **WHITEPAGES.COM** was a the right name, with a Florida address but, NO PHONE NUMBER. NO EMAIL. What to do? Write a **LETTER** – a novel concept in the technological world in which we live today.

It was refreshing to write a "friendly letter" – the kind that we were taught in school, oh so many years ago. I asked for the recipient to please contact me by phone or email even if he wasn't Sylvia Englander's son. Usually, I can count on the mail delivery taking about a week cross country. To my surprise, I received a telephone message AND an email within four days. Cousin Ted was most interested in learning about all of my discoveries and wanted to share them with his brother, Dave, who had also retired in Florida.

Elizabeth Ruderman Miller

Within two weeks, I had located three male cousins and their families to add to the Family Tree. I was thrilled that the male members of the family were so enthusiastic to learn about our family connections. Some other male cousins had shown very little concern, if any at all. There were no disappointments, no rejections, only open arms and excited voices, each wanting to participate in this wondrous journey which I have taken over the last years. I look forward to meeting EVERYONE. Life at 60 was very rewarding, indeed.

Israel Connection

In the mid 1960's, our family had a visit from Tuvia Hofnung, mom's cousin from Israel. He spoke very broken English with a heavy accent, and I recall being aggravated by his personal campaign to encourage all American Jews to live in Israel. I was a teenager looking forward to my college years, and I had no designs on travelling out of the country yet, let alone volunteering in the Israeli Army.

Following the death of my Dad in 1983, I agreed to accompany my Mom on a two week visit to England and Israel. My insatiable interest in ancient history had not yet evolved. Since I had been a Theatre Arts major in college, I was more interested in seeing some British theatre productions.

Not only were we to visit our Israeli relatives, but we would spend time with old family friends from Pennsylvania, who were raising their Orthodox family in Jerusalem. I was fascinated as I compared and contrasted the religious vs.

Zionistic views of this tiny country which was so often the center of contention regarding world peace.

I had seen pictures of my twin cousins, who were the daughters of Tuvia and his wife, Yaffa. Ora and Sarah were a few years older than I – both were married and also raising young families. Regardless of their very limited knowledge of English, their children were learning the language in school and assisted us with Hebrew/English translations during our conversations. We 'broke bread' with our family at their home in Tivon, and it was on that evening that I learned about Tuvia's connection with the fight for the State of Israel, his earliest journey to Palestine and the fate of his family in Poland.

Sarah Borensztejn, sister of Chana Yetta, Ruchel and Abram Borensztejn, married Arie Hofnung and lived in the shtetl of Gritse, Poland. The surviving Borensztejns, children of my great grandparents, Dina and Tuvia, remained a close-knit group even after immigration or deaths, **(as was the case of several sets of twins, stories told to me during my youth by my Grandma Annie**); most probably, my twin cousin, Sarah was named for her grandmother, Sarah, following Jewish tradition.

Sarah and Arie Hofnung had four children. At fifteen, looking to escape the atrocities in Poland, their son, Tuvia journeyed to Palestine. After his initial stay, he returned home to encourage his parents to bring his siblings to the Holy Land. When they agreed to join him, Tuvia traveled back to his newly adopted home. I couldn't help the feeling of intense pride and gratitude which I felt for Tuvia, when I learned that he had been a brave member of the Haganah, the underground military organization prior to the establishment of a Jewish homeland. Tuvia fought beside the likes of David Ben-Gurion for the statehood of Israel. I did find it a bit odd, however, that at the dinner table, along with Tuvia, Yaffa, their children and grandchildren, was his former girlfriend and compatriot who had shared many of the war experiences, nodding her head in affirmation as the stories unfolded. When I chose to question certain specifics about his experience during this turbulent time, I was informed that certain information was better left unsaid. This type of secrecy is perhaps why the Israeli intelligence has such a worldwide reputation.

The Haganah was founded in June 1920 in Eretz Yisrael (the Jewish homeland to be established in the general area of Palestine) as an independent defense force completely free of British authority. In the beginning, the Haganah defended larger towns and settlement. After the Arab riots of 1929, the design status of the Haganah changed dramatically. It became a large organization encompassing nearly all youth and adults in the settlements as well as several thousand members from each of the cities. It initiated a comprehensive training program for its members and ran officers' training courses. The Haganah established central arms depots into which a continuous stream of light arms flowed from Europe while simultaneously, laying the basis for the underground production of arms.

As a result of the British government's Anti-Zionist policy, the Haganah supported illegal immigration and organized demonstrations against the British policy.

After the outbreak of World War II, the Haganah did head a movement of volunteers from which units were formed to serve in the British army. It cooperated with the British intelligence, sending members on commando missions in the Middle East. Jewish parachutists dropped behind enemy lines in 1943-44. All the while, the Haganah further strengthened its independence by instituting basic training for the country's youth. Haganah branches were established at Jewish displaced person camps throughout Europe. Members accompanied the 'illegal' immigrant boats. During the spring of 1947, with the preparation for an impending Arab attack, David Ben-Gurion took it upon himself to direct the Haganah general policy. Finally, on May 26, 1948, the provisional government of Israel decided to transform the Haganah into the regular army which is today the Israel Defense Forces. [4]

The German army overtook Gritse on September 12, 1939. One of Grandpa Sam Hiller's nephews was the first person shot and killed while he was crossing the street.

4. "The Haganah," The Jewish Virtual Library, A Division of the American Israeli Cooperative Enterprise

This was **verified** by my cousin, Benjamin who was the only member of either side of my family to survive the Holocaust.

Sadly, the Hofnung family was unable to depart Poland before their capture by the Germans. It's unclear as to the year of Sarah Borensztejn Hofnung's death, but I suspect that she died prior to her family's apprehension. This deduction is based on **my discovery of THE PAGES OF TESTIMONY,** records located in the **Central Database of Shoah Victims' Names at YAD VASHEM,** in Israel. **In memory of his family who were murdered in the Shoah (Holocaust), Tuvia had submitted four pages – one each for his father, Arie, his brothers, Moshe (born 1913) and Menakham (born 1926) and his sister, Tzira (born 1916).** The material does not include the year of and place of death, and my suspicion is that either Tuvia did not have that information, or perhaps the Hofnung family lost their lives from hunger or an epidemic in the Grojec ghetto.

After Tuvia Hofnung's death, Mom had been out of touch with his family in Israel. Through **The JewishGen Family Finder,** I visited the page looking for any researchers who were interested in the town of Grojec, the Polish spelling for Gritse. I sent several emails to people in Argentina, Germany, France, Canada and received the following uplifting message about my Israeli cousins on October 5, 2006:

"Liz Shalom:

I found your family in Tivon. They were very happy to hear from you. They promise me to contact you. I spoke with Ora… one of the twin girls. (supplied address and phone number) Good luck, and I was happy to help you. By the way, we may have a family connection? I see you married a Miller. With my best regards.

B. Miller
Haifa – Israel

The following morning, I received an email from Ora's children whom I had met in the mid 1980's with my Mom. Anat and Ran were now both married with children. We continue to chat via email and telephone. Anat became my family genealogist, supplying me with the entire Israeli family Tree, which, I'm happy to say, continues to thrive.

Last, But Certainly Not Least

Finding three of four missing family branches is very exciting. Still, I was determined to locate the last of my Grandfather Morris Ruderman's brothers, Harry and at the very least one of his descendants. I WAS RELENTLESS. Harry's face was identified on the **WEDDING PHOTO** from 1938, however, no one remembered anything additionally about him or his wife and family. I was starting from scratch. Having been previously challenged, I knew I was still up to the task.

Since I had so little information on Harry Ruderman, this would prove to be my most methodically directed search of all. I began with his name and perused the **latest U.S. Census, from 1930**. I assumed only one fact: since all of my Ruderman acenstors lived in the meltopolitan area of New York City, especially Manhattan and Brooklyn, Harry and his family may have as well. I might have been proven wrong, but you must have a launching point, and this was mine.

Many Harry Rudermans later, I was struck by one listing on the **ANCESTRY.COM 1930 UNITED STATES FEDERAL CENSUS.** Harry and Gussie Ruderman lived in Brooklyn and had six children. Their first born son, Samuel, age twenty – five appeared along with his other siblings – Sarah (Sadie), David, Esther and Abraham appeared to have been born in New York. Lacking sufficient information to formulate additional assumptions, I checked the **1920 UNITED STATES FEDERAL CENSUS,** only to discover that **Samuel and his parents IMMIGRATED together in 1905.** Samuel was born in **ENGLAND!** Two records – two pieces of contradictory information. Still, I wanted to complete the Census search by viewing the first Federal Census in which I hoped Harry and his family would have been counted – **1910 UNITED STATES FEDERAL CENSUS**. Harry's estimated birth date of 1883 was almost exactly identical to the other two census reports. Golde was a very acceptable woman's name of it's day, yet, she changed her name to Gussie sometime prior to the 1930 census. Living with them were two men who had recently immigrated and were reported to be Azer Shapiro, Golde's brother and Hirah (this name was misread and was actually Hirsh) Ruderman, Harry's brother. As yet, there is no paper trail for either man, except for the **Ship's Manifest** showing their arrival. There may yet be another Ruderman brother

How Will I Know Where I'm Going, If I Don't Know Where I've Been?

from Kraisk in the United States; that proof will have to wait for a later time. The important detail which appeared was Golde's maiden name **SCHAPIRO.**

My choice was to explore the **SOCIAL SECURITY DEATH INDEX** on **GENEALOGY.COM** which produced eight results for Harry Ruderman in New York. Only two of the **birth years** fell in the correct time period. This site provides an **AUTOWRITE LETTER**, which you can send, along with a payment to obtain a copy of someone's U.S. **SOCIAL SECURITY ACT APPLICATION FOR AN ACCOUNT NUMBER** containing valuable information including address, employer, date and place of birth, social security number, signature and **FATHER'S AND MOTHER'S FULL NAMES**.

Harry was born on January 12, 1882 or possibly 1883; he applied for a Social Security number in 1937 at the age of 54; and most importantly, his parents were identified as **Isaac and Ruth Lily Ruderman.** The name Lilly was a complete surprise to me (perhaps Abe's daughter, Lillian was named for her). Ruth can easily be translated into Ruchel or Rachel. **AH-HA!!**

A CERTIFICATE OF DEATH can be secured from the **Division of Records, Department of Health** in New York City. About a month after mailing my payment, I received the document confirming that Harry's mother's name was Rachel, and that Harry was buried in the well-known New York cemetery, Montefiore on Long Island.

The **1920 U.S. Federal Census** showed Harry Ruderman's family living on Gates Avenue, Brooklyn. His **World War I REGISTRATION CARD** dated September 12, 1918 confirmed that he and his family lived at 611 Gates Avenue and provided another important fact about which I compare in a future document. Harry was self-employed as a carpenter.

ANCESTRY.COM has resources for the **ENGLAND AND WALES FREE BMD (BIRTH/DEATH/MARRIAGE) INDEX, 1837-1915.** I pulled up a Samuel Ruderman from the first quarter of 1905 registered in **Newcastle Upon Tyne, Northumberland, Tyne and Wear County, England.** Newcastle is in the northern section of England. I did not know how to request forms from England, so I posed a question on the **JEWISHGEN. ORG SIG (SIGs are the Special Interest Groups which offer information on geographic, regional or special topics on the Jewishgen.org website.)** and received two responses, one from the United Kingdom and the second from Denmark. <u>Genealogy research is a very global and socially interactive exercise now that we have internet websites</u>. One person even went so far as to confirm that Samuel Ruderman was actually born in November 1904, but the birth, for whatever reason, was not registered until the family departed for America in early 1905.

How Will I Know Where I'm Going, If I Don't Know Where I've Been?

I wrote to the **GENERAL REGISTER OFFICE** in **ENGLAND,** charged my seven pounds ($15.00), and subsequently received an **Official Certified Copy of an Entry of Birth** for Samuel Ruderman, born to **HARRIS RUDERMAN and GOLDE SAPIRO ON TWENTY-EIGHT NOVEMBER 1904**.

Interestingly, Harris (English for Harry) Ruderman's occupation is listed on the his son's birth certificate as **Master Cabinet Maker,** a very good match for the carpenter which was shown in the census record. If I could discover their immigration records and establish why they delivered their son in England and stayed for at least four months, I would truly have a complete portrait of their journey and the beginnings of the (Harry) Ruderman family in America.

Genealogical research is a step by step process. There are days you are itching to find the next good clue which will allow you to solve your mystery. Be patient. Take advantage of all sources and keep asking questions.

Sometimes it is hit or miss. No matter how hard I tried, I could not find the **Immigration Records** for **Harris, (or HARRY) GOLDE or SAM RUDERMAN.** An email arriving on July 28, 2008 miraculously changed all of that. Another **JEWISHGEN** researcher (we are all researchers, professional or amateur) wrote:

> "Son of a gun! I did a search for all the males ages 22-28… using **Steve Morse's Gold Form** and couldn't find Harris either. But, then

Elizabeth Ruderman Miller

> I decided to do a search just for **Shapiro,** and I think I found him (Harry) as **EISIG SCHAPIRO!** He had been living in England (same as Golde's manifest). It says he's a **cabinet maker,** so I think this is really him… I think he is eleven pages ahead of Golde (on the manifest). **YOU WOULD THINK THESE PEOPLE WOULD REALIZE THAT WE WERE GOING TO BE LOOKING FOR THEM YEARS LATER AND WOULD USE THE NAMES WE KNOW THEM BY! <GRIN>"**

How very clever of Barbara, the researcher, to look for the wife's maiden name. That taught me a very valuable tool for other searches. I logged into **ELLISISLAND.ORG,** typed in Golde Schapiro and there they were – numbers twenty-one and twenty-two: Golde Schapiro and her son, Sam; last residence: London. Eisig Schapiro, the married cabinet maker appeared several pages later. All three arrived in New York on March 20, 1905 having sailed on the S.S. Saint Louis out of Southampton. **The JEWISHGEN GIVEN NAMES DATABASE** confirmed that **EISIG** was the Yiddish equivalent of Harry.

I have no idea why all three family members travelled under Golde's maiden name. I was very satisfied with my efforts and the volunteer research which enabled me to find this long, lost relative. It was now time to attempt my last, but not least search for Harry and Gussie's descendants if at all possible.

The SOCIAL SECURITY DEATH INDEX listed Samuel Ruderman, born on November 28, 1904 (which I knew to be the correct information) as having last resided in St. Louis, Missouri. With the date of death, February 8, 1997, I wrote to the **Missouri Department of Health** requesting a certified copy of Sam's **Death Certificate.** When it arrived, the death certificate contained all of the information which I would need to verify that Sam was a member of our Ruderman family.

The **Death Certificate** contained Harry and Golde Sapiro Ruderman's names. I believe that Sapiro was the Russian spelling for what we know as Shapiro. His dad's profession was that of cabinet maker and painter, so it was logical to see that Sam also was a painter in St. Louis. He married Rose Levy, whose family I later learned had lived in St. Louis where they owned a Boot/Shoe Shop. How did Sam end up in St. Louis? Perhaps he and Rose met in New York, where the Ruderman family resided. After tracing all known records of Sam and Rose Levy Ruderman, I was never able to locate any children born to the couple. By contacting the **St. Louis Genealogical Society,** they were able to confirm the birth and death dates for husband and wife and their burial location of Chevra Kadisha Adas B'Nai Israel in Missouri. I also **retrieved a copy of the**

obituaries for a small sum from the **St. Louis Public Library.** Libraries and historical societies are excellent sources for historical information, so don't leave them off of your research lists.

The next eldest son was David Ruderman. Using the **Census Records from 1910, 1920 and 1930,** I knew that David was born between 1908 and 1910. His **death certificate,** pinpointed his death as November 1980, if those were the correct records. Again, I ordered a copy of the **APPLICATION FOR AN ACCOUNT** with the **U.S. SOCIAL SECURITY DEPARTMENT.** David Lewis Ruderman was born on January 16, 1909 to Harry and Gussie Shapiro Ruderman. When he applied for his **Social Security number,** he was twenty-eight years old and unemployed. However, in 1930, the **Census** states that he was a painter, like his father and older brother. Perhaps the ravages of the Depression caused his unemployment during 1937.

David's **Certificate of Death** clearly states his date of death, November, 26, 1980. His parents, Harry and Gussie Shapiro Ruderman were also mentioned. Of important note was the reference to Pauline Ornstein as the maiden name of David's wife.

With these names, I again delved into the **Italian Genealogical Website** for **New York City marriage** between 1929-1937 in the borough of Brooklyn. There are times when you can find the groom's records or the bride's records separately; luckily, in the case, I found them both. Pauline Ornstein and David Ruderman were married on September 24, 1932. I was able to obtain an official copy of their **Marriage Certificate,** for a nominal fee. Through this paper, I was able to verify all of the facts I had discovered. This document, along with the other certified records, would become important official accounts of my Ruderman family history. I hoped that they would be pleasant surprises for David and Pauline Ruderman's sons, Herbert and Steven and their descendants.

You need to use the powers of deduction when looking for some information. I decided to pay for a 24 hour pass to **INTELIUS,** a People Search Report which lists current and historical people who may share the same name and state as your search subjects. The People Search Summary can provide a consolidated view of matching records for your subjects name across multiple public sources. I was able to cross-reference the information on the website, **PEOPLEFINDERS.**

I copied a three page report with names relating to Herbert Ruderman after discovering a listing in the **SOCIAL SECURITY DEATH INDEX.** With several choices, I selected one and called the number. The young woman on the other end of the phone, although surprised, was very willing to speak with me. She confirmed that Herbert was her father-in-law and told me a bit about her family. She confirmed that 'Uncle Steve' was Herbert's brother, and that I did have his correct telephone number.

I dialed Steve's number and was greeted with "Sorry, I don't take telemarketers calls!" I was taken aback, but this was not the first time I had experienced rejection. I was, however, determined not to fail at making a family connection, so, I redialed Barbara, Steve's niece, just to ask her if she would <u>please</u> tell 'Uncle Steve' that I was for real. Within an hour my phone rang, and it was Steve, my long lost cousin in Florida. He apologized for his initial rudeness and was quite delighted that I had found him. Of course, neither of us had knowledge of each other, and unfortunately, he knew nothing about his grandfather, Harry. It was my pleasure to copy and send him all of the documents which I had found about Harry and his descendants. He photocopied some black and white pictures of his dad, David, brother, Herb and himself taken during the summer of 1950, in, of all places, Monticello, New York, in the Catskill Mountains about twenty-five minutes from my home in Port Jervis!

Nine months later, in April 2009 on a trip to Florida I was able to visit with Steve and his lovely wife, Brenda. We looked through old photo albums together, so that I could familiarize myself with some more Ruderman faces. I questioned Steve about the summer trips to Monticello. He explained that his father, like his grandfather, was a house painter. During their summer getaways from New

York City, David still needed to work to bring in money for the family. He took several painting jobs in Port Jervis. I couldn't believe that David never knew he had a first cousin who was a Pontiac dealer and an Uncle who was the butcher in Port Jervis in 1950. Perhaps, they may have met, but a union NEVER produced a family bond between the families. Steven and I are exactly the same age, and it would have been nice to have known each other all of these years. We continue to stay in touch via email and phone and look forward to another reunion in the future.

I did locate some additional records for Harry and Gussie's other children and grandchildren. As yet, I have been unable to make contact with any additional family members. Their daughter, Esther married a Lawrence Goodman on July 12, 1912. They had two sons, Michael and Harold, who may possibly be deceased.

Sarah/Sadie Ruderman married a Joseph Horowitz but with so many Joseph Horowitz listings and no Sadie Ruderman in the **Brides or Grooms New York City Marriges** to correspond, I have reached an impass, but hope to discover a connection in the future. Abraham Ruderman is also an extremely prevalent listing, so I will need additional research time to locate the youngest of Harry and Gussie's children.

Connecting with my cousins (during the summer of 2006) has been more fulfilling and joyful than I could

Elizabeth Ruderman Miller

than I could have imagined. I have spoken on the phone with Ellen Fenster, Barbara Gardetz and Carol Rothman, Ted and Dave Englander and Mimi Bornstein. I've had the please of seeing Pam and Bob Hoffman and their wonderful family and Ronda Ruderman twice. My initial visits with Mark Kresel, Steve Ruderman and Robert Bornstein leave me with hopes of seeing them in the future and meeting their families. My once tiny little family has grown, and I know I have family all over the United States and abroad.

It was *B'SHERT,* (Yiddish for meant to be; destined) that I would take this enlightening Genealogical journey. First, my Mom shared details with me that she may not have even thought about or remembered earlier in my life. If the websites and the enormous amount of information were not available on the Internet, I can't fathom the difficulty I would have had, let alone the years it would have taken, to have attempted this project earlier. It was the right time and even the right place for me. It was b'shert. I have had the most extraordinary experience and the time of my life.

Epilogue

My accomplishments came, first and foremost from the deep passion which evolved when I finally asked, "Who were my ancestors?" I was never looking for anyone famous hidden in my genealogical records. I did, however, want to put myself in the very old shoes of my family members who toiled during the mid 19th century, or earlier if I were to be so fortunate. I'm a dreamer, a traveler, a sleuth, an actor, a story teller and a teacher. As with my former students in the classroom and in life, my wish is that my journeys, stories and historical accounts will inspire readers. Anything can happen if you put your whole heart and soul into the project.

This will undoubtedly be a lifelong work in progress. The next phase of my unending research will be a tour of my Russian homeland with my husband and hopefully several cousin/friends accompanying us on the journey.

Who knows what our detective skills are capable of finding?
ANYTHING IS POSSIBLE!

RUDERMAN

SIBLING VERIFICATION THROUGH PARENTS' NAME CONNECTION

MORRIS RUDERMAN –	ISAAC RUDERMAN RACHEL AXELROD	1903 MARRIAGE CERTIFICATE
ABE RUDERMAN -	ISAAC RUDERMAN RACHEL AXELROAD	1908 MARRIAGE CERTIFICATE
SOPHIE RUDERMAN –	ISAAC RUDERMAN RACHEL AXELBROAD	1907 MARRIAGE CERTIFICATE
HARRY RUDERMAN -	ISAAC RUDERMAN RUTH LILY AXELROD	APPLICATION FOR ACCOUNT NUMBER U.S. SOCIAL SECURITY
ESTHER RUDERMAN KASDIN –	ISAAC RUDERMAN ROSE (UNKNOWN)	CERTIFICATE OF DEATH NEW YORK STATE 1948

COMPARISON OF BIRTH LOCATIONS OR RESIDENCE

MORRIS RUDERMAN –	GRYSK, VILNA, RUSSIA -	DECLARATION OF INTENTION FOR NATURALIZATION
ABE RUDERMAN -	KRAISK, RUSSIA -	PASSENGER RECORD ELLIS ISLAND
SOPHIE RUDERMAN –	KRAISK, RUSSIA -	PASSENGER RECORD ELLIS ISLAND

HARRY RUDERMAN -	RUSSIA only -	APPLICATION FOR ACCOUNT NUMBER U.S. SOCIAL SECURITY ACT
ESTHER RUDERMAN - KASDIN-	KREISKE, RUSSIA -	PASSENGER RECORD ELLIS ISLAND

RESOURCE WEBSITES

GENEALOGY AND LINK SITES

www.jewishgen.com

www.ancestry.com

www.familysearch.org

www.myheritage.com

US, FEDERAL AND UNITED KINGDOM

www.stevemorse.org

www.nationalarchives.gov

www.nationalarchives.gov.uk/census

www.findmypast.com

PEOPLE FINDERS

www.intelius.com

www.ussearch.com

www.zabasearch.com

www.whitepages.com

www.stevemorse.org

www.peoplefinders.com

OLD MAPS
- www.avotaynu.com/maps.html
- www.bklyn-genealog-info.com

PHOTOS, DIRECTIONS AND CURRENT MAPS
- www.mapquest.com
- maps.google.com
- gis.nyc.gov/doitt/mp/Portal.do
- Earthgoogle.com

RECORDS IN OLD COUNTRIES
- www.rtrfoundation.org
- www.jewishgen.org

MILITARY
- www.anestry.com
- www.footnote.com

OLD CITY DIRECTORIES
- www.uscitydirectories.com

NEW YORK CITY RECORDS
- www.newyorkgenealogicalandbiographicalsociety
- NYGB

FAMILY AND SOCIAL NETWORKS
- www.facebook.com
- www.myspace.com

NAME TRANSLATION
- www.jewishgen.org/databases/GivenNames/search.htm

Made in the USA
Lexington, KY
10 April 2010